song of the sparrow
NEW POEMS AND MEDITATIONS

MURRAY BODO, O.F.M.

ST. ANTHONY MESSENGER PRESS
Cincinnati, Ohio

Cover design by Mark Sullivan
Cover collage by Randel Plowman
Book design by Jennifer Tibbits

LIBRARY OF CONGRESS CATALOGING-IN-PUBLICATION DATA

Bodo, Murray.
  Song of the sparrow : new poems and meditations / Murray Bodo.
     p. cm.
  ISBN 978-0-86716-864-8 (pbk. : alk. paper)
  1. Meditations. I. Title.

BV4832.3.B63 2008
242—dc22

                                  2007040382

ISBN 978-0-86716-864-8

Published by St. Anthony Messenger Press
28 W. Liberty St.
Cincinnati, OH 45202
www.SAMPBooks.org

Printed in the United States of America
Printed on acid-free paper
08 09 10 11 12 5 4 3 2 1

contents

To my brothers at Pleasant Street Friary:

Jack Wintz
Dan Anderson
Jim Bok
Greg Friedman &
Mark Hudak

introduction

I began the original edition of *Song of the Sparrow* with these words:

There is something ragged and unfinished about sparrows; yet they have always endeared themselves to me. There is something Franciscan about their simplicity, their habit-colored feathers, and their availability when other birds hide away in the woods or fly south for the winter. This book is sparrow-talk, becoming song from time to time. I hope it is simple and unaffected song like the song of the sparrow.

It is over thirty years now since I wrote those words of the original edition of *Song of the Sparrow* in my room at Saint Francis Seminary in Cincinnati. A morning person, I wrote at night, that being the only time I had to myself after a day of teaching and an evening of listening to high school seminarians tell their stories in the sanctuary of spiritual direction. My experience as a seminary English teacher and spiritual director informed much of the first *Song of the Sparrow*.

In 1977, the year after *Song of the Sparrow* was published and twelve years after being assigned to Saint Francis Seminary, I was transferred to Duns Scotus College, our Franciscan undergraduate seminary in Detroit, as professor of English and director of young friars. Two years later Duns Scotus College was closed, and I was transferred back to Cincinnati's inner city where I have lived ever since. The intervening years, 1979 to 2007, make up the section, "Summer," in this new edition, *Song of the Sparrow: New Poems and Meditations*.

In 1977 I also began spending summers in Assisi, Italy, as a pilgrim guide for what became known as Franciscan Pilgrimage Programs. Nothing has so affected my writing life as have the thirty years of summers on pilgrimage to Rome and Assisi. Many of the meditations and poems of "Summer" were inspired by these pilgrimages to Assisi, the beloved city, my muse.

In 1988 I began doctoral studies in English at the University of Cincinnati, receiving my degree in 1992. That journey, too, is here: the wonder of it, the disciplined reconnection with poetry and fiction, with in-depth pilgrimages into Henry James, William Faulkner, Emily Dickinson and other writers, modernist and contemporary. From my undergraduate years on I'd been influenced by the clean, spare style of Ernest Hemingway, the mysticism (which he'd no doubt deny) of T.S. Eliot, and the Franciscan wonder and Scotistic theology incarnated in the poetry of Gerard Manley Hopkins.

To reenter the worlds of words in my fifties was a great grace and reinforced my love of English and American literature, its human (and at times divine) depths, its power to transform and prepare the soul for grace. It was in the study of literature as a young man that I was prepared for the study of sacred Scripture. The word prepared me to receive the Word; literature gave me a way into the Word of God, its profundity, its varieties of structure and genre and expression. That story is here, too, at least indirectly in the words that fill the pages of "Summer," which was written in the fiftieth year of my life as a Franciscan friar, my seventieth year to heaven.

The remainder of the book is pretty much intact, except for refinements here and there and for the inclusive language that was not a part of my consciousness and writing in 1976.

I hope these words are still sparrow-song, more ragged at the edges, perhaps, but filled with gratitude. This new *Song of the Sparrow* tries to sing on like an aging bird whose voice is less insistent, less knowing, a bit intermittent, but still reaching for a full-throated song.

AUTUMN

a walk in the woods

A WALK IN THE WOODS. THE AUTUMN RAINS HAVE TURNED THE leaves to mulch beneath my feet and black trees are slowly emerging from their green cover of leaves. Thought-time again. In summer prayer comes with difficulty in the heavy-hanging air, but with fall as the leaves rush down, our thoughts rush heavenward again. Perhaps it's our own mortality we see in autumn leaves, perhaps it's the clearing of the skies that were blocked by green foliage. Whatever it is, fall brings with it a clearing of the mind and heart, and we look up and out of ourselves for a Presence whose hands hold the life that will lie hidden till spring.

What is this prayer of fall? Mostly it rises from an emptiness caused by nature's dying into winter. And in a sense this emptiness, this longing to live, is the beginning of all prayer. I walk in the bleak November woods and I want to believe that I am not alone, that this loneliness is illusion only. And so I reach out and call upon God and I am no longer alone. For there behind the wet, behind the black trees, behind my own feelings, is He who walked the same earth and entered into its dark soil only to rise again, opening forever the dark recesses of the earth and of the human heart. And I thank him and this too is prayer.

I AM SITTING IN A HIGH-BACK ROCKER LOOKING AT THE LARGE MAPLE tree that fills my whole window with its leaves. And this staring becomes part of prayer. Who can pray who does not make time for staring out windows? Prayer requires time, and time we jealously hoard for what we consider most important in our lives. Perhaps time is for recreation or work or sleep or watching TV. I usually can tell what is really important to me by the amount of time I am willing to spend on it. And if I am willing to "waste" time on something, it is usually because I have done it before and found it worthwhile.

This previous satisfying experience is important to any prayer life that will endure. I must have experienced somewhere, sometime, the presence of God, or at least a faith in the presence of God in my life, in order to long to meet God in prayer. I must have found sitting in a rocker pleasant and relaxing if I am to return to it often. The more fulfilling the experience is, the more I will be drawn to repeat it.

Fulfillment, of course, is a tricky, loosely used word; and if I place too much emphasis on my own fulfillment, I will pray only when I foresee or experience some personal satisfaction. But if my fulfillment comes from rendering to God what is God's despite my own feelings at the time, then justice and duty will prevail; and I will continue prayer throughout all the seasons of my life. Fulfilling my obligations to the good God will satisfy my own need for fulfillment in the long run, whereas seeking my own fulfillment will not ultimately fulfill my obligation to God or to myself.

> OUT OF the heart
> the song rises,
> the mind searching
> for notes
> to capture
> its flight.

REMEMBERING THE MOUNTAINS OF MY CHILDHOOD IN DURANGO and Silverton, Colorado, I sit down and dream. I see them again the way they closed out what was ugly beyond them. They were always forming deep gorges and valleys where you could walk and fish, sealed in by 12,000-foot peaks that made you feel secure and unafraid of anything except perhaps the mountains themselves, but that was in the wintertime. And the whistle of the little narrow-gauge train never seemed an intruder but a contact with a world you wanted to be "out there" as long as you didn't have to live in it, and it stayed a comfortable distance away.

I HAVE BEEN A FRANCISCAN FOR OVER FIFTY YEARS NOW, AND THIS fact makes me think once again of the vows and their significance in the life of a friar. Unfortunately, they sometimes amount to nothing more than a commitment to "hang in there." Surely, an impoverished idea of the vows, but perhaps sufficient to get us over the rough spots. All vows, however, including marriage vows, have to amount to a lot more than that. They should be a commitment to grow into a new person in Christ, and they should be made with this transformation into Christ as their chief motivation. I must, in making my vows, firmly believe that I am entering into the work of God, that I am entering upon a long process of purification and liberation to which God has called me by name.

If my vows amount to nothing more than hanging around friaries and wearing the habit, or hanging around home and a marriage, then certainly they are a mockery of everyone's fundamental call to grow in God. And if after giving up my previous home, family and everything for Christ with one side of my mouth, I then gradually call it back with the other side, vows themselves can become little insurance policies guaranteeing a comfortable, mediocre life of non-involvement with God or a spouse and fellow human beings.

Unselfish love and transformation into Christ are both the motivation for and the purpose of vows. And this love and Christ-likeness is also the measure of how well I am living my vows. I try to live my vows with God's help, and God works the transformation with my help. For no vow to God is one-sided. God promises literally everything in return for my gift, and God is faithful.

> THANK YOU, Lord,
> for your support.
> Without you life is
> impossible and becomes a contest
> of personalities, in which the strong
> and self-assured always win.
> When the weak and despised and unlearned
> prevail, then I know you are working
> and not the self-will of human beings.
> Only your Spirit is wisdom and only
> they are wise who open themselves to
> that Spirit and surrender to your Father's
> will. Come, Lord Jesus.

OUR LIVES ARE A FORGETTING AND A REMEMBERING. A RHYTHM that follows us relentlessly till death. We are alive and doing and we try to forget the fears and anxieties about the future which paralyze us in the present and make us dead and inactive. We are people who hope and believe and so we try to remember the good that God has done for us. We recall God's faithfulness and care, and we become men and women of the future who dare to act because we forget our failures and remember God's action in our every thought and deed. We stay sane because our eyes are on God who loves us and proves it when we dare to live for God. If we remember to remember God, we find our lives are meaningful and free.

THE PRESENCE OF GOD IN YOUR LIFE. YOU CANNOT MERIT SUCH AN experience; and even if you are not aware of God's closeness to you but continue to do God's will, God dwells within you. Yet, you still long for God to speak or reveal that God is there. Is this selfishness? I don't think it is because this longing is something beyond your control. Turn wherever you may, nothing and no one short of God can satisfy your longing or distract you from that gnawing in the mind and heart which speaks of an emptiness yet to be filled. Your faith says that in heaven longing will cease and every tear will be wiped away. But that future seldom suffices to make the present any less painful. And so you continue to search for the living God.

All of us who turn to God, at one time or another ask if God really exists. Are we only deceiving ourselves in order to give meaning to our own unfulfilled life? And then subtly, in ways we did not expect, God comes to us fleetingly to keep alive the longing and the hope of the resurrected life to come. God never comes on our terms but in God's own time and place, and God's appearance is often a surprise. No one ever sees God, of course, but we see the shadows of God's passing through our lives in the things that change which we never thought would, in the prayers that are answered in ways that we never expected, in a new level of maturity that we know we couldn't have arrived at alone. And once again our faith is enkindled, and we begin to hope for more, for a sound in the air, for a sign unmistakable and clear.

God is a lover and leads us artfully, attracting us, then showering us with blessings, then withdrawing to start the process all over again on a new level.

THE PRIMACY OF FORGIVENESS. UNTIL WE LEARN TO FORGIVE DEEPLY and sincerely, we remain only on the threshold of real union with God, we remain essentially imprisoned and unfree. In the course of a lifetime, we gradually accumulate countless little resentments which, if allowed to grow, become big hates and seemingly insoluble differences. As we know, whole nations can grow to hate and mistrust one another. If, however, we do not allow these jealousies and hatreds to grow, but instead try always to purify our hearts, we enter into the mystery of love, the mystery of God.

We have so much to forgive: life, maybe, certainly those who have hurt us and even ourselves (perhaps most of all, ourselves). Often we are hardest on ourselves and need to forgive ourselves for failing, for being less perfect than we would like to be. God forgives us much more readily than we forgive ourselves, and this inability to forgive ourselves is the cause of much of our pain and inability to grow.

Forgive, then, and we will begin to live. When Jesus said, "Love your enemies," it was not so much for our enemies' sake as for our own. When we hate, we become small and petty, and the worm of decay eats at our hearts, and the taste in our mouths is bitter. But when we forgive and love those who persecute us, we grow big and surpass even our own imaginings of what we could become. Love is expansive and its taste is sweet in the mouth.

GIVE THANKS TO THE LORD ALWAYS AND YOUR LIFE WILL BE A SONG. Some songs are sad, of course, but the melody is still there as well as the movement and the feeling of freedom that come from music. To praise and thank God, no matter what happens, is a gift that few possess. To lift your voice and heart on high in failure and defeat places you among the saints; for only faith and love can explain a song of praise and thanksgiving when times are bad.

trusting

TRUSTING GOD. SELF-CONFIDENCE AND CONFIDENCE IN GOD ARE so closely connected that we can confuse one with the other. Sometimes when I say I have lost my trust in God, I really mean I have lost confidence in myself. Or when I say I have no self-confidence, I mean I have lost my trust in God's care for me. When all is going well in my life, I usually have boundless confidence in myself, and perhaps I don't even think of God.

These thoughts raise the question of how much each of us fashions a God to fit his or her own personality. In thinking about this question and noticing how many people have a God different from mine, I realized that though God is God, we experience God differently. The basic revelation is constant and more or less the same for all believers, but the God who is experienced is different because God is experienced by different personalities. At the beginning of faith, especially, God is revealed to each one of us as the kind of person whom we can love and adore. That is why a straightlaced person has a straightlaced God and a flexible person's God is understanding and tolerant.

The only assurance of some common idea of God is the church, but even the church does no more than ensure an orthodoxy of ideas about God. The church reveals to us *our* God. But the living God who is experienced is still personal in the sense that God is *my* God, who lives and acts in my life, and who is grasped and knows my unique personality. *The* God who is, is universal and unchangeable. The God who is known by me is unique to me. How I see God changes through the years as I change and come to know the one true God more and more as God is and not as I experience God.

Ultimately, of course, God as God is never wholly knowable by human beings, no matter what names or concepts we use to describe or try to define the eternal I AM. Often what we say about God says more about us than about God. We know God only by the effects of God's existence and presence and by what God has chosen to reveal to us.

HOW MANY THINGS HAVE WE HIDDEN AWAY IN OUR MEMORIES, afraid to look at them, to bring them to the surface and disarm them by facing them and seeing that they are not as bad as we thought? And if we look at them with Jesus at our side, it is easier still because they are healed by his sharing the memories with us. We are sometimes so successful in suppressing what we do not want to remember that to our conscious mind the experience is as if it never happened. But it smolders beneath the surface, burning little holes in our will when we want to do something and find we cannot do it. If we let Jesus share these memories with us, they lose all their power to scare us into inactivity. And this healing process frees us from the past.

ONE OF THE DISTURBING THINGS ABOUT GROWING OLDER IN THE service of God is that I sometimes feel that I know God no better now than when I was fourteen, and the fifty-plus years intervening have not been fruitful of a deepening awareness of God in my life. But I regard this sort of thinking as a temptation, mainly because I *have* persevered for all these years. No one, I feel, can persevere in God's service or in any sustained love without God and without God's constant working.

Some of the other experiences of my life are more intense at times, but they are sporadic and short-lived. I do not experience God in my life the way I experience the presence of people I love, but everything I do and everything I am presupposes God dwells within me and makes possible my other loves. That is perhaps sufficient for anyone, and anything beyond that is superabundant gift.

THE FRANCISCAN CHARISM IS ULTIMATELY TIED UP WITH LOVING those who are seemingly unlovable or who return love with hatred and contempt. Saint Francis, in reaching out to the leper, paved the way for his followers to walk. And like Saint Francis, when we let God lead us among those who are seemingly repulsive, our love eventually makes them beautiful and they become a source of sweetness and joy to us. This is not because we are patronizing them or "doing good" but because *we* are changed inside and begin to see people as they really are in God's sight. Our vision is cleared of our own prejudices and dim perception. For only love opens our eyes to what is really there.

The tragedy of those who don't have charity is that they project their own failures and ugliness onto others and think that the evil and imperfection inside is really outside them and resides in people and situations they can't stand. And that is what it means to be spiritually blind. It's hard to see anything but splinters when there's a beam in your own eye.

Writing is a form of therapy; sometimes I wonder how all those who do not write, compose or paint can manage to escape the madness, the melancholia, the panic fear which is inherent in the human condition.

—Graham Greene

THE LOVE OF GOD. WHO CAN MEASURE ITS DEPTH AND BREADTH? Is it not those who are poor and weak and call upon God as their only support? When all else fails, sometimes only then, we realize we are dependent creatures who live and grow only in God.

Some long to know that truth experientially but cannot. They know they are weak and in need, but their only dependence is on what they can see and hear and feel. They want to believe that God is there: independent, all-knowing, all-loving. But they cannot make that jump, and they wonder why a God who is supposed to exist doesn't help them see, help them make that jump.

This is a mystery. Why do some possess that inestimable gift of faith through no apparent merit of their own, and others who long for it stand empty-hearted and bereaved? The mystery lies somewhere in the center of the statement, "God is love." Love chooses not to force. Love does not push us into things. Love invites, and we respond. To all appearances the jump is absurd, a risk we take that involves all kinds of human faiths that precede divine faith. We dare to believe that when we pray, we are not, in fact, talking to ourselves but that someone actually hears and answers. And the biggest step of all, is when we accept that Jesus Christ is the Incarnate Son of God, himself God and coequal to the Father. To top it off, these invitations to faith are sometimes offered by people who may seem fanatic or at least a bit crazed by some strange illusion that they are different from others, that they are people possessed by God.

Those who have been born into a family of faith find the leap of faith fairly easy, but those whose background is nonreligious find this world of faith a strange world indeed.

WHEN GOD ALLOWS SORROW AND AFFLICTION TO COME INTO OUR lives, God always has a timetable different from ours. God asks us to bear our cross for a certain period of time and nothing we try to do seems to lift that cross from our shoulders entirely until we are transformed and God is ready to elevate us to a new level of love. God is never the author of evil, but sorrow and affliction are not necessarily evil; they can prove to be for our own good, not just in eternity but here and now. God can, of course, bring good even out of evil, as Saint Augustine says. But what I am mainly talking about here are those little neuroses and disabilities and anxieties that come into our lives and which we try desperately to understand and rid ourselves of, sometimes for years on end. And then one day they are no longer there and we find ourselves ready to meet life, more humble and trusting in the goodness and providence of God.

From these painful visitations that God permits we grow, and we come to know that they were good for us even though we did not understand why when they were upon us. And strangely, past experience does not seem to make the next cross any easier, though in some there is a positive acceptance of God's will that makes even suffering a walking with God that has its own kind of joy. In all of this those without faith often see a masochism or self-hatred in this kind of acceptance of suffering. That can be there, of course, but it need not be. It is all in the heart and mind of the sufferer, and only God knows that.

MORE VALUABLE THAN ANY LOGIC OR PROOF FOR GOD'S EXISTENCE demonstrated in books is a personal experience of God. People of prayer and interiority know God mainly through God's *working* in their lives. They have known God in the prayers that were answered, in problems and in difficulties overcome that only the power of God's Spirit can explain, and above all in the charity of their lives that transcends human patience and love and reaches a level of selflessness that faith alone makes possible.

The witness of a selfless God-centered life, therefore, is the greatest proof of the existence of God. People find God in people who have already found God and live in that love.

ONE OF THE DEEPEST SOURCES OF JOY IS THE AWARENESS OF healing taking place inside us. When we have been ill or depressed or confused and afraid, we pray mightily for deliverance. And then one day we notice that something is happening, that our health of mind or body is returning. And this steady growth of strength and peace within us is like a new birth, a new chance to live again.

That is what happens to us in the sacrament of reconciliation. Our sins are forgiven as soon as we confess them and are absolved, but the healing is a gradual process. Gradually and imperceptibly we are being made whole, and then there comes a moment when we realize that something wonderful has happened to us. What before seemed impossible is now possible and what was previously so difficult is now somehow easier.

Most healing of the spirit is effected only when we verbalize our hurt, when we say to another that we have sinned or that we are troubled deep inside. The sacrament of reconciliation provides that kind of divine healing. And it gives us the opportunity to listen as well. We listen to the Word of God and to the words of the priest and we pray with him for healing. Everyone needs healing, and to neglect an opportunity like the sacrament of reconciliation is to let pass one of the most effective ways in which we grow from inner sickness to health.

I LEAN ON GOD, BUT FROM TIME TO TIME I FEEL THAT I AM LEANING on air. That happens when I start putting God out there somewhere too far removed from me. When I remember that God dwells in me and in all my brothers and sisters in Christ, then that leaning becomes substantial again and God takes flesh in those around me whom I can see and hear. We are the body of Christ, and he has no other visible body here and now. God is Spirit who has become enfleshed in Jesus and Jesus takes on flesh and bone in us through the same Holy Spirit. When we lean on one another, we are building up the body of Christ. We are strengthening our own weakness by acknowledging that we are only a part of the whole body and that we need all the other members if we are going to function correctly and appreciate our own worth. By leaning, we stand upright and God becomes real for us because we are no longer trying to be our own strength. Christ marrows in us.

DO WE MAKE ORDER WITH WORDS? DO WE FIND, AS ROBERT FROST says, some momentary stay against confusion in the well-made poem? In the making of a poem, in the doing, there is the order that comes from the discipline imposed by words. Words, properly arranged, are the essence of our thinking. When we are confused, our words are confused. And if we cannot sort out our own confusion, we can at least try to create or discover order in words on the page. In ordering these words, perhaps my own thinking will become clear or at least clearer than it was before I put them down.

I KNOW THAT THE LOVE OF GOD MUST HAVE FIRST PLACE IN MY LIFE. And when I let it slip behind any other love, there is tension and confusion in my heart. All other loves, if they are not second to the love of God, become stumbling blocks to my own growth and inner freedom. If I am to be free, then God alone has first claim on my heart. My time and preoccupation must be with doing God's will, with pleasing God. This lesson is learned daily, and each new love is a challenge to this simple truth: All loves are purified in the love of the God who made love.

ONE SECRET OF THE LIFE OF PRAYER IS THAT WE MUST LEARN TO PRAY without a sideward glance to see if anyone is watching. We must, as Jesus counsels, go into our room, close the door, and pray to our Father in secret. This entering into our room and closing the door is something we must do even when we are praying in public, even when we are praying with others, and maybe especially then. Otherwise, like King Claudius in Shakespeare's *Hamlet,* we cry out,

"My words fly up, my thoughts remain below, / Words without thoughts never to Heaven go."

If our words are calculated to please others or to impress them, or if we use our prayer to bolster our own egos before others, then our thoughts remain below. Our concentration must be on God, who lifts us up and out of ourselves. If our thoughts during prayer are truly on God, then we will be accepted and admired by others. For then, and only then, will we be independent enough of our fellow human beings and dependent enough on God to be truly ourselves. And when we are truly ourselves, we are loveable enough to be loved.

SOMETIMES I CANNOT SLEEP AT NIGHT BECAUSE GOD IS STIRRING MY soul. I have no direct experience of God, but my restlessness and tossing makes me rise and take pen in hand to record my own weakness and God's great love and kindness. Praise God who acts in our lives when we think it is only our nerves or our inability to unwind and let nature take its course. When we rise and do God's will, we sleep well the remainder of that time we call the night.

THE LOVE OF GOD. HOW LITTLE IT IS UNDERSTOOD OR BELIEVED. So many people do not believe that they are loved or loveable. And yet God sent the Son to identify with each one of us in an unbelievable act of love. Perhaps that "unbelievable" is why many can't believe. Maybe it is incredible that we are so wonderful in God's eyes that God would go this far to impress upon us our own worth. But if we can accept the fact of this love of God for us, we regain our self-respect and dignity and walk free as sons and daughters of God.

SOMEONE ONCE TOLD ME HE HAD TAKEN UP SKYDIVING BECAUSE HE had no reason for not doing it except that he was afraid, and he did not want to start not doing things simply because he was afraid.

How much good is left undone and how many dreams and hopes are shattered for lack of courage? Fear can steal into our lives so subtly that we might not even recognize it at first. We may think it prudence at first, or good sense. But ultimately it shows its ugly head for what it is, a killer and a paralyzer of action and of the fulfillment that comes from doing.

HOW HARD IT IS TO SLOW DOWN AND LET THE HEALING HAPPEN when the very sickness is a fear of slowing down, of not being able to function as well as we could, of paralysis of will. Healing is most impossible when we cannot forget the sickness long enough for healing to start.

PRACTICALLY EVERY CHRISTIAN BOOK ON PRAYER IS SIMPLY A commentary on the Lord's Prayer. Jesus' own formula for prayer is *the* model of how we should pray. All true prayer should take us out of ourselves, out of the narrow confines of our self-conscious preoccupation with our own thoughts and feelings. Jesus' prayer does that immediately: "Our Father, who art in heaven." We are out of ourselves, addressing our Father, calling upon God as our Father. And this other-centeredness continues: "Hallowed be thy name." God's name defines and is synonymous with who God is. And we pray that this name will always be held holy. Reverence, respect, adoration of the One we are daring to address. "Thy kingdom come." Praying for God's kingdom to come is saying yes to all of salvation history and yes for all that is yet to come in the plan of God. And then perhaps the hardest prayer of all: "Thy will be done." God's will! To say yes to that is to accept the totality of what has happened, is happening, and will yet come to pass as it is willed by the Father. And that means suffering and sorrow as well as happiness and joy. This whole first part of the Lord's Prayer has been addressed to the Father and has been wishing for God everything God wants from us: That God be our Father, that God's name be holy, that God's kingdom come. And that the Father's will be done. And we pray for all of this not to *My* Father, but to *Our* Father because we are one with all humankind whose common Father is our personal Father as well.

Only then do we pray for ourselves and all others. "Give us this day our daily bread." We trust in our Father's loving providence to care for us from day to day. We live and pray in the present and God answers our present needs, not those future needs we imagine are coming. "And forgive us our trespasses as we forgive those who trespass against us." No prayer is possible without forgiveness. We must forgive those who offend us if we are to expect God to forgive us our offenses. A heart that cannot forgive is a closed heart and God will not enter there. And so we pray with Saint Francis, "And if we do not forgive perfectly, Lord, make us forgive perfectly." "And lead us not into temptation, but deliver us from evil." We acknowledge our fallen nature and our dependence on God. Only in God can we be victorious over evil, and only a humble awareness of our need for God will keep us from succumbing to temptation. For God's is the kingdom and the power and the glory forever. As we began with praise, we end with praise; and everything in between flows from that praise. Very simply, that is what prayer is all about.

IN FALL THE TREES TURN AND THE SKIES CLEAR AND I REMEMBER New Mexico. One of the most enduring of my childhood memories is the bright blue of New Mexico's skies. Even the memory of that blue clears my mind. I don't remember the trees turning when I was a boy, but their turning now is a signal that a little bit of New Mexico will be transported here to Ohio: The leaves will fall and I will see the sky again. On a clear day I am renewed as I am at other times only when I am on the beach listening to the sea sing.

The sky and the sea: the two symbols of my life. My childhood was all up and away into blue heavens and my adult years were a constant finding and losing the sea. As a child I wanted to escape into the beyond; as a man I am always looking toward my origins, toward the seas from which I came. The two, sky and sea, are the tension and the balance in my life.

TRUE LOVE IS RELATIVELY FREE OF EMOTIONAL DEPENDENCE ON THE beloved. And this includes the love of God.

signs of god's presence

JEREMIAH. ALWAYS BEFORE ME, PROPHET WHO SPEAKS PERSONALLY TO my heart. You, Jeremiah, in your vocation, make my own vocation real. Your vocation is the prototype of every vocation. Without you, I would give up and say it is foolish to serve God this way. But because of you I know I was called before I was born, that God cares enough to send even you, even me, to be God's mouth and broken body and crippled mind. And we listen because God speaks through the most improbable instruments. They who seem to be God's instruments, but really aren't, speak words that last only for their own lifetimes because they are their own mouthpieces and the message dies when they do. They who speak for God live forever in God's Word, which outlives the instrument of its speaking.

THE HEALING POWER OF GOD. RARELY DO WE REALIZE THE HEALING power that is going on inside us. We do not notice it because we mistake it for something else, we mistake it for an evil. If we have learned to enter into prayer, then we see with new eyes and hear with new ears. And what we perceive is that what we previously thought was surely some scourge of Satan in our lives, is in fact the healing hand of God leading us through the fire of suffering in order to purify and heal what only suffering *can* heal.

We never love the suffering, and it is not lessened by our new consciousness, but our *faith* is strengthened because we begin to see connections and patterns in our lives. We see that each new pain, each new difficulty leads us to a new level of maturity and healthy dependence on the God who loves us. Why this growth must come through suffering is a mystery, but we know that the mystery is somehow inseparably linked with the cross of Christ. Only one who has accepted the reality of the cross and its redemptive power can ever accept the fact that suffering is growth, that paralysis is movement on another level. Only in the mystery of the cross are T.S. Eliot's lines intelligible: "Suffering is action and action is suffering."

What more can we say of suffering? How do we explain, for example, the terrible pain and suffering some bear in this life though they pray for healing, and no healing comes? To me there is something inscrutable about physical pain and suffering. We know that in the Gospels Jesus wants to heal and we have many instances of Jesus healing physical illness. In fact, Jesus always heals those who are brought to him for healing.

But what about those who were not brought to Jesus, what about those who were not healed during Jesus' lifetime though he walked among them? Is it only that they were weak of faith, that they were those of whom Jesus said, they are of little faith? Or was it, is it, God's choice that some suffer and are ill, and some are not? Does God, then, choose evil for some? That cannot be, for God is all good and all loving. And so the problem of suffering and pain and illness and how God fits into it all, is again inscrutable.

One can say that illness is built into the very essence of reality as we know it. What is born and dies experiences pain and illness as a part of what it means to be a living being on this earth. But then does God create an imperfect world, or did something we did or do make it so? Again, we go round and round with inscrutable questions, and the only answer seems to be Jesus, God's Son, who suffers and dies like us—as if to say, there is no answer, there is only this, my own willingness to suffer with you and as one of you.

When we suffer, then, we know it is a mystery why it should be so. But because of Jesus, when we are suffering and/or dying, there is also Jesus' invitation to ask for healing; and if it is not forthcoming, to join with Jesus in his suffering and dying, certain in doing so that if we suffer and die in him we will rise in him, as well. That, it seems to me, is where we place our faith even when we are not healed or those whom we love are not healed.

POETRY WORKS TOO POWERFULLY ON ME TO SUBMIT MYSELF LIGHTLY to any poet. It is like friendship. I have to trust before I love. Most people I know start with love. I love poetry as an abstraction, but individual poems grow on me as I learn to trust the poet through his or her poem; for the poem is the poet and what is said is who is saying it. Some sayings are unreliable. I look for the transcendent in the particular. Particulars in themselves tend to be self-serving and convoluted. Only the transcendent, the metaphysical, frees the particular concrete experience from the poet's own introversion.

THE REAL SIGNS OF OUR FAITH ARE OFTEN THE MEN AND WOMEN WE know. Some are evident signs of faith, hope and charity, and others are signs of contradiction. It is the latter people who disturb us and make us question whether we are seeing things aright. Those who are hostile and aggressive and speak like self-righteous prophets, make us wonder if they are real. The meek and humble somehow beguile us by their gentleness and littleness.

TRYING TO WRITE SOMETHING EVERY DAY IS LIKE TRYING TO PRAY every day: You have to discipline yourself to it because there are always more "important" things or more fun things to do. But if you steel yourself to setting time aside, things begin to happen while you are in the process of writing or praying. Flannery O' Connor once said, "Every morning between nine and twelve, I go to my room and sit before a piece of paper. Many times I just sit for three hours with no ideas coming to me. But I know one thing: If an idea does come between nine and twelve, I am there ready for it." That quote is one of the most perfect descriptions of what happens in prayer that I have ever seen.

For me prayer and writing often go together. But even if they don't for someone else, the process of the two is much the same. I must be willing to sit before a blank piece of paper, as it were, if I am ever going to learn to pray. Time for staring and time for waiting. Patience to wait for God to act, for God to speak. If I expect something tangible to happen inside me every time I pray, then my prayer has become superstition or magic. All I have to do is utter certain formulae and God appears like some genie. If this were the case, God would not be God, but some puppet of ours. And God *is* the Lord, God *is* God.

Therefore, I make myself available to God and I pray. God will come when God will come if I persevere in prayer, just as the idea comes and "happens" on the paper if I persevere in writing. Inspiration comes while I am in the process of putting words on paper, and God comes while I am involved in that process called prayer.

I write even when I am tired. It reminds me to pray even when I'm tired. With both writing and prayer there is something to show afterward. Not much usually, but enough to make me glad I did it, if only because God is my witness.

freeing the spirit

THE TROUBLE WITH SELFISHNESS AND GREED IS THAT IT SLIPS SO easily from material things to things of the spirit like reputation, or honor, or appreciation and fame. And this need to hold onto adulation slips sooner or later into a kind of slavery to other people's opinion of us. This whole process turns us increasingly inward; and ironically, it makes us insecure and fearful. So that what began as an ego-building enterprise, like building the tower of Babel, ends in confusion of tongue and heart that makes us afraid to say what we mean or to mean what we say.

On the other hand, selflessness and material generosity flow from and into spiritual freedom. And this free spirit leads us unerringly out of ourselves to God who is perfect freedom and in whom and for whom we move with the uninhibited freedom of a child. We become aware that we are children of a God who loves us with a Father and Mother's love, and everything we do becomes a gift for God, to please and thank God for being who God is to us. Gradually, the negativism and disapproval of life's persistent critics means little at all when compared to our determination to do the will of the One who made us and redeemed us. Even our occasional ignorance of what that will is, is purified in our intention to do it as best we can.

WHAT I ADMIRE MOST IN A PIECE OF WRITING IS THE FEELING THAT I am reading something said well, that I am reading someone who has something to say and who has mastered the craft of putting ideas and/or images down on paper so that they stick in the mind. This craft does not come easily. And as I try to stumble through my own writing, I grow daily in my admiration for what goes into the making of a great work of literature. At times the making seems more important to me than the finished work itself.

The same holds true when I meet someone who is genuinely holy. I say, "My God, the self-sacrifice and surrender to God's will that must have gone into everything this person is!" And where the person has come from and the journey getting to this point become more important than what he or she is. This is especially true for people because, unlike works of art, they are never really finished; they are ever in the process of growing or regressing. And holiness means that they are growing more than they are regressing; and though growth is the nature of all loving things, growth in selfless love is not natural to fallen human beings. Only the power of God's Spirit and our surrender to it can explain a steady growth in charity. That process is more wonderful than any other creating I know of. The greatest art is the art of entering into that death and resurrection cycle we call redemptive love.

TO LOVE GOD WITH OUR WHOLE HEART AND OUR WHOLE SOUL AND our whole mind. What does that mean? Does it mean, for example, that there is no love left for anyone other than God? Such a love would be absurd for a human being. And what is inhuman is surely not Divine. My love for God must be whole-hearted and God must come first, but in and because of God all my other loves are purified and actually made possible. The more I love God, the more human I become, for I am made in God's image. My humanity mirrors the One who made me. If on the other hand, my love is primarily for the church or my work or someone other than God, I begin to lose my humanness, for I have set up an idol in the place of my Creator, and I begin to resemble the idol. My humanity is tied closely to divinity, for to be human is to be like God in whose image I am created. The more God-like I am, the more I am myself. But the more myself I am does not necessarily mean the more God-like I am. For often in striving to be myself, I can be setting up another idol, namely a false image of who I think I am. I find myself in God, but I do not necessarily find God in finding myself. The self cultivated can end up being the most pernicious of all idols. But the cultivation of the love of God invariably leads to the greatest possession of myself.

I HAVEN'T WRITTEN FOR A WEEK OR SO. TOO MANY DISTRACTIONS, too much work to do. Funny, I haven't prayed as much either. God's subtle reminder that I have to make time for God.

WHEN I COMPARE MYSELF TO OTHERS, I HAVE AN IMMENSE SENSE OF failure, of inadequacy because I see only their strengths which seldom are my strengths. But when I forget comparisons and look only to what needs to be done, what can be done, I am at peace in the knowledge that I have something to give, something to offer. If I give of myself, it will make a difference, even though someone else could have given more, could have loved more perfectly, could have succeeded where I failed. If only everyone realized that the gift she or he can give is unique and does make a difference! What pain of self-pity he or she would be spared! We can never be the people we admire. We can only be ourselves, and that alone is admirable.

MAY MY GIFT BE ACCEPTABLE TO YOU, O LORD, FOR IT IS ALL I HAVE to give. May my gift be acceptable to you, my brothers and sisters, for it is the same gift I offer to God: myself, my love.

IN THE night
Alone with my thoughts
I remember you, O God;
And my empty room
And emptier thoughts
Are filled with your
Love, your watchful care.
And loneliness is changed
To praise, to gratitude
That empty hearts
Are lodges for your
Loving presence.

WHY IS IT SO HARD TO TALK OR WRITE ABOUT GOD WITHOUT sounding general and full of platitude and cliché? Isn't it because our experience of God is so personal that to talk about God's love sounds like self-celebration, sounds as if we are making ourselves special souls upon whom God has lavished love? Or is it because we really don't know if God is present to us in a personal way and so we repeat what Scripture says God is supposed to do? For my own part, my book on God would be my own autobiography, because I don't know God apart from what God has done for me, through me, with me and in me, and in all those I've known in my life.

I CONFESS MY SMALL INSECURITIES, O LORD, BECAUSE OF THE ONE BIG security of you.

I WONDER AT TIMES WHY I KEEP A NOTEBOOK. WHAT COMPULSION makes me put pen to paper day after day? Is it because I hear in my heart some intangible voice that says someone may find you, O Lord, in an entry that I took time to write down? It is that way with all our acts, really. In you they somehow have a deeper, more lasting significance than our mere doing them would seem to warrant. And your words about the cup of water offered to the very least of our brothers and sisters echo in my mind. Nothing is ever lost on you, Lord. You grace all our goings and all our smallest touches of love with your redemptive power. We sanctify everything we touch and, sadly, we seldom know we are redeeming and deifying creation by a mere smile. All of this once seemed sentimental to me, but then I suppose we do move from our spiritual adolescence into the childhood of maturity.

WE RELEARN THE LESSON OF DETACHMENT WITH EACH NEW STRAW we clutch at in the wind. Funny thing about straw in the wind: We never forget that it is only straw, but when nothing else is left to cling to, straw has all the attraction and beauty of a messenger sent from God to give us new life and love. And so, deceived again, we reach out and try to build something solid with straw. And it dries up and blows away before our eyes, and we learn to wait for God who sends the wind and the straw to see if we are ready yet for God. Our reaching out for any straw says that we are. And God comes the minute we let the straw go without regret and with remorse for thinking God could be content with our choosing something less than Love.

> CONTRITION ALWAYS comes to me when I realize
> How hard I've been trying to avoid living with
> So elusive a lover as God. It brings with it a
> Wry sense of how hard it is to live without God, as
> Difficult as God can be sometimes. And something deeper
> In me makes me smile and say to myself that God is worth it.

> Morning breaks each time you come, O Lord.
> And night picks up the shattered pieces of dawn

And glues them together whenever you go away.
I live in a vase broken and glued so many times
It has its own sentimental value for me.
And inside the darkness of the vase I see so many cracks
That each new breaking is easier. Even I can do it now.
You used to have to break it from the outside.

Some people say if you wait for God, nothing will happen.
I don't believe that. A lot happens that you don't want to
    happen,
And so you say nothing has happened when you
mean, nothing you wanted to happen came to pass.
Surrender to what God is working within you, and every-
    thing
that happens shines with your own unique light.

I write easiest at night when everyone else is asleep.
I pay for it dearly in the morning when everyone
else is awake.

I WRITE LITTLE POETRY WHEN I DON'T TAKE TIME FOR STARING OUT
windows or walking through the woods. And prose is so much easier to write, at least for me. The self-discipline, concentration and
contemplation necessary for poetry are ironically luxuries in my life
instead of the necessary stuff of a friar's life that they could be.

TO PERSEVERE IN ANYTHING IS NO MEAN ACHIEVEMENT, BECAUSE IF
you persevere to the end, you have to persevere from day to day. If
you are faithful in the end, you were faithful all along the way. It
seems to me that nothing is ever achieved without a certain daily
doggedness that comes from a conviction about what you are working for and toward. Nowhere is this more evident than in prayer, for
the daily fruit of prayer is at best a vague sense of peace, but more

often that not, it is merely a sense of having tried. However, from time to time there is the breakthrough of God that is worth the daily drudgery and is, I think, only possible because of the daily perseverance that preceded it.

Not that you merit a breakthrough because you persevered, but a certain attitude of receptiveness and patience, of humility and longing grows imperceptibly but surely in the heart of anyone who prays regularly in season and out. And the cumulative experience of your prayer reinforces the conviction that prayer, after all, *is* communion with the God you cannot see, so that in the end you are secure in having "known" God. You may not be able to put your finger on any one experience of God, but you will say that God found you in prayer, in your life-long endeavor to pray.

> WALKING THE leaves down
> On an autumn afternoon
> I feel it again, that brown
> Mulching of the spirit,
> and I sense a settling in
> For winter, a searching
> For caves and nests in
> Cozy corners of my heart.

WITNESSING A YOUNG FRIAR MAKE HIS VOWS, I THRILL AT WHAT HE is doing. I look back on my own years vowed to God, and I know something of what he will endure and the joys he will have. Everything he experiences from now on will either be a fulfillment of or a challenge to Saint Francis' motto, "My God and my all." Discovering what those words mean experientially will be the warp and woof of the pattern his own life will reveal in the end.

Each friar discovers for himself what that "all" means. And every false god that creeps into his life will evoke a response from God, who, when the friar least expects, will lead him gently or not so gently out into the desert of purification to remind him that he is in fact a pilgrim, a wanderer, nomadic and bent upon a heavenly city.

I SIT and listen for your voice, O Lord,
And the silence of the trees is what I hear.
I look for your reflection in the lake
And I see white clouds mirrored there.
I reach out for you and feel the air.
And then I remember that you are Spirit
And my own spirit breathes you in.

ON THE feast of Saint Francis 34 years ago,
October 4, 1974, the poet Anne Sexton
Was found dead at the wheel of her car,
The engine running mechanically well.

THE DAYS OF MY YOUTH SOMEHOW ARE MORE VIVID IN MY MEMORY than those of the immediate past. So much so that I often feel like the young boy I was. Perhaps this is more than memory. Perhaps we are always aware of our growing, of our moving toward something rather than our having arrived. To the child the adult seems to have arrived somewhere; to the adult the child seems a mirror of himself or herself.

This kind of experience in me may only reveal that I have not really grown up yet, or it may mean that my awareness of myself is only as strong as my most vivid memory of myself when I was most impressionable.

WE DRIFT AWAY FROM GOD SO EASILY; NOT FAST, BUT EASILY. AND before we know it, we are far downstream from God trying desperately to break our acceleration and reverse our direction. The water is always too fast at that very point, and God draws us back with a strong hand; that is, if we're trying to row with God.

HOW GOOD ARE YOU, O LORD. YOU SURPRISE ME WITH YOUR HELP and your love when I least expect it, and you make it all good again—the suffering and pain, the loneliness and fear, the helplessness and despair. And when you come, I forget the way it was without you, so compelling is the power of your presence. Nor do I fear your leaving, for when you are with me, only you occupy my mind, I rejoice because the Bridegroom is here.

But you do leave me, or so I feel at times, and in the darkness it is hard to remember the light. If, however, I begin to see the pattern of your coming and going, of darkness and light in my life, then I acquire a peace and tranquility of heart. I gradually learn that nothing in this life is forever. And with this insight I don't despair when you withdraw nor do I presume that your felt presence will remain when you draw near.

What remains is the pattern of your coming and going and that in itself is proof enough for me of your presence in my life. The movement of your Spirit, Lord, is like the wind: It blows where and when it will and no magic of mine can conjure it up or make it disappear. And that is all I need, Lord, to know that you are God, that you are independent of me. Your love alone moves you to come to me. Your will be done.

WHEN MY MIND BEGINS TO DARKEN AND MY SHIVERING HEART longs for something more or something other, writing helps because in the magic of words seeking each other and rubbing their surfaces together gently, a warmth emerges until, striking each other sharply, a flame is struck from their surfaces, revealing some hidden fire within. And when it happens, though it's happened before, it is a surprise. I merely brought the words together, trying different combinations and discarding those soft words that haven't enough flint for sparking. And if I am lucky enough to strike a fire, my mind is lit up and my heart is warmed; and others who read the words, join me at the fire. And there around that fire civilization continues.

I DON'T WRITE A BOOK; I FILL ONE PAGE OF A YELLOW LEGAL-SIZED pad each day. Neither do I achieve sanctity; I just try to do God's will each day. In both cases what happens eventually depends on whether or not I remember to work at it every day. If I do, God will supply the rest.

rainfall and
night thoughts

THE WAY THE RAIN HIT MY WINDOW THIS EVENING AND THAT
sudden opening of clouds awakened something inside me, and I was
back in Assisi on a rainy afternoon thirty years ago. The same fullness
was there inside me. From time to time something in the landscape
or the weather leaps out at us, and we feel that we have been here
before, that time is being somehow reversed; and even if we don't
remember what the past experience was, we relive the feel of it.

I sometimes think heaven will be that way. It will be a new experience, but something about it will awaken the feeling that somewhere in another life we have experienced something like this new-
ness. And it will be good, both in itself and in the remembering, for
surely we are increasing our enjoyment of heaven even now. In coop-
erating with God here and now we are in a sense preparing part of
our own heaven. In heaven there are many mansions, but we move
into those mansions with our own experiences, and the fuller, the
more perfect those experiences are, the greater will be our capacity
to be filled with God, who though infinitely beyond our experience,
will not destroy our memories of meeting God on earth.

THE QUIET OF THE NIGHT. SOMETIMES, SLEEPLESS, WE LISTEN TO THE
sounds of the night and count the hours with all-night TV or radio
shows. Perhaps we should turn off the TV and radio and listen to the

sound of our own hearts beating faster than they should, and in the quiet of the surrounding night, lift our minds and hearts to God whose calm heart paces the universe.

That sounds good on paper; but whenever I try it, it fails to produce either sleep or rest. And so I count on sleepless nights from time to time as being part of the human condition. And I remember Jesus spending whole nights in prayer and try to imagine him, like me, a human being with a human being's problems and fears. Then sleepless nights don't seem so bad, and they are even peopled with hundreds of others who cannot sleep. And strangely, I sleep much better just knowing that; for what often keeps me awake is the thought that everyone else is asleep.

LIFE IS FULL OF AMBIGUITIES AND UNANSWERED QUESTIONS. YET WE survive, we continue to find pleasure and joy in the smallest things. We struggle with some temptation, some problem that plagues us and makes our days heavy and our nights broken and troubled. And then for a few minutes or an hour some small surprise (a piece of music, a card game, a visit from an old friend, a scent of roses in the air), and we are temporarily drawn out of ourselves into something other.

Life should have its little surprises. When there are no more little joys, no more surprises, our own pseudo-sophistication is killing the life within us: and it is time to become like little children again. The ambiguities and questions will be there no matter what we do. The little surprises will be there only if we want them, only if we expect them to come, and that is hope. And that sustains us.

THE ONE CONSTANT: GOD IS LOVE AND FAITHFULNESS. UNTIL WE realize that God really does care, we are without faith. No assent to truths or dogmas ever substitutes for a deep, personal conviction that God loves me and cares about what happens to me. If I have all knowledge, Saint Paul says, and have not charity, what difference does it make? And charity, Saint John says, is this: That God first loved us and sent his Son to redeem us. Saint John complements Saint Paul.

The King James Version of the Bible puts it all together when it says, "Believe on the Lord Jesus." Yes, only if we believe on him, does dogma and church and sacrament and all the rest make sense. For from Jesus comes the church and what it teaches and what it symbolizes in outward signs. Never does faith begin with something other than God. God initiates and everything else follows from that. And God did initiate the church through Jesus, the Incarnate Second Person of the Blessed Trinity, and from that church everything else derives. To love the church is to love Jesus and to love Jesus is to love God, for Jesus is the enfleshment of God.

In the end, then, God's love and faithfulness is revealed once and for all in Jesus Christ. And that the love of Jesus is manifested on this earth and continues after his resurrection in his followers, is the greatest proof of all that God does love and that God is faithful now—in the past—and presumably in the future, as well. If I know that God cares now through Jesus, I believe God cared in the past, too, and my hope is firm that God will care in the future.

joy in god

HOW GOOD ARE YOU, O LORD! WHETHER YOUR HAND LIES LIGHTLY or heavily upon us, it is your goodness that moves you to touch us. And we know you by this touch, this action in our lives. Something happens that we don't expect, and we find ourselves growing in a way we didn't think possible or didn't even imagine existed. And we know that you have touched us again.

ALWAYS IT IS THE SAME: YOU SUDDENLY REALIZE THAT GOD HAS BEEN there all along, that yes, God is present in your life. And the words of praise and thanksgiving rise to your lips, perhaps after great sorrow or suffering or that darkness of mind which seems endless and terrible when it is upon you.

And what is it that brings that realization of God's all-loving presence? Isn't it that something changes inside you that cannot be explained by anything you did or anyone else did to you or for you? Often something you have been hoping for or praying for just happens. Perhaps you wake up one morning and something is different. You accept what you couldn't before, or you look in the mirror and laugh at yourself. And peace seeps through your whole being, and everything seems good again in spite of pain or sorrow or loss.

JOY IN GOD IS NOT EASILY WON, IF IT CAN BE SAID TO BE WON AT ALL. Joy is a gift from God, one of God's surprises that comes to us when we are expecting something else. And yet we can also say that joy is won. It is won by those with heart enough to surrender to God. God gives the power to surrender, but we alone can choose to use that power. So in that sense we win our joy in God. And "win" is a good word here, for the surrender is never made without a struggle; and in this case by losing the struggle against God and surrendering to God, we win! Another paradox, another reality that only the Spirit of God can explain. Only in the power of God's spirit is our defeat our victory, and our surrender our real possession.

> ALONE ON a wintry night
> the wind ticks
> against my window
> like nature's clock
> reminding me of time
> passing.

WHO KNOWS WHAT LOVE IS? AND HOW MANY WHO KNOW EVER SAY? Most of the love I have known has been non-verbal. It has been there in devotion and duty and fidelity revealed in peoples' lives. It has endured when words have failed. It has sustained me when no one knew what to say. And always behind all love has been *the* Love, Yahweh, Lord, the God of all. I've never seen or heard God. Nor have I known God as the saints and mystics have. But I believe God is here with me. And that is love, and all I know about it.

Others, I am aware, experience the presence of God as surely as they experience other people. And from that deep faith they put to shame those like me who walk mostly in darkness, envying those whose God lives experientially within them. What keeps me going is praying for that kind of knowledge. I want it and would trade anything for it. That, too, I hope is love. For if it is not, then there is no room in heaven for those who search and cry out in the night for the smallest light to see by.

O LORD, listen to me, your poorest of lovers.
I come to you, as I always do, begging.
I am not ashamed to beg from you, Lord,
For you are the source of everything I have.
I see people starving everywhere,
And that is what makes me ashamed to put
My poor petition before you.
Help them first, Lord. My suit can wait.
When they are satisfied, I will ask you to turn
To me. In the meantime, remember my
Frailty, Lord. Being more filled than
They, I am more vulnerable to temptation,
More apt to turn elsewhere for what you
Alone can give me. And I'll remember
Always that you are big enough to pay
Attention to us all: the famished of body
And the famished of spirit, as well.

TAKE ME in hand, O Lord.
Though your palm be rough,
I will not shrink if only you
Manhandle me before I
Seek smoother palms and
Softer touches than yours.
I've known your firm grip
And your blows and they are
Touches of love more sure
Than any caress or soothing
Stroke of lover's tenderness.
And always it is you who man
Me again when my own
Soft heart unmakes your
Strengthening virility.

WHEN THE HEART REBELS AND SAYS, "I WILL REACH OUT FOR LOVE wherever it may be found," and the mind echoes, "Yes, and I will not see," and the conscience says, "I don't care anymore," then memory rises like a bright and redeeming sun and says, "Yes, but you have been here before and God saved you in the nick of time. God comes if you ask just one more time, remember?" And again it is memory that cries aloud, "God is faithful and will not abandon those who trust in God." And the past is made present through memory's alchemy. This saves us time and again, and we praise and thank God who gives us the past to make the present a wise and redemptive future.

I LOVE you, Lord.
But to say it here
Seems to cheapen it.
Maybe that is just my
Own reluctance to
Profess love too loudly
And regularly in print,
For outside of written
Words I'm always saying,
I love you. Funny thing
About the written word: what
We say always in everyday
Life when put down on
The page doesn't work.
Art is suggestion, is under-
Statement, is not saying
What the reader would say
You said even if you
Didn't say it.

CAN WE EVER GIVE THANKS ENOUGH FOR ALL GOD HAS DONE FOR us? We begin to understand what thanks means when we stop comparing ourselves to others and look at what God has done for us. God loves me in my uniqueness. God applauds when all other hands are still; when my own heart doubts my worth, God becomes my audience, an audience of one who is more important than many.

Is this illusion? If it is, then saints do not exist and our own experience is illusion. For we all know men and women for whom God alone matters in the end. They live and die for God, and everyone else they touch is freed by their selfless love and their own detachment from the obsession to succeed in human terms. They accept human praise and human love, but their world does not collapse when it is withdrawn. Behind everything is the good God who stands in the wings and claps when there is silence from the gallery and boos beyond the footlights.

And so we bow bravely whatever comes our way knowing who stands behind us, clapping for our effort and laughing when we take ourselves too seriously. Thanks then rises to our lips as naturally as to a performer who has just brought down the house.

I THINK ONE OF THE REASONS I WRITE IN THIS JOURNAL IS BECAUSE IT keeps me from writing poetry which is always so inward-reaching and at times so close to madness. Here it is easier. You let the thoughts find themselves, and the emotions are sufficiently remote to make the act of writing safe. Most of the discipline of a journal is in making yourself write every day. The discipline of poetry is in the long silent periods of seeing and hearing and distilling in the mind and heart—then in trying to get it down on paper in tight, controlled images. No wonder I prefer these daily scratchings of the surface of the mind.

the one who is there

GOD IS NEAR. NO WORDS BRING WITH THEM SO MUCH CONSOLATION and hope as these and so much despair when they seem not to be true. God is near. That is precisely what everyone wants to believe and what so much of our experience seemingly belies. Perhaps God is so far from us sometimes because we don't recognize God, or because we have already decided what those words mean. They mean that what I need more than anything else in life will be there. Usually that means love or intimacy of some kind. Rarely is it suffering or pain that we anticipate when we expect God to be there. And surely it cannot mean emptiness, loneliness, absence; for that is the very opposite of what we mean when we say that someone is near us or someone is there when we need him or her.

But God is not just anyone, and God's presence is often so much like absence that only one who has learned quiet and prayer would ever recognize God in the empty air that neighbors every one of us. Nor would that empty feeling in the heart ever lead the non-interior person to break through the emptiness to that fullness which is sometimes surrounded by the protective shield of the void. The fullness of experience in God comes clothed in the disguise of absence, and only prayer can see beyond the disguise to the One whose nearness is as close as our feeling of God's absence. With God absence and nearness are complementary terms in the sense that it is hard to distinguish one from the other. Furthermore, a feeling of nearness can mean that God has become my own emotional euphoria at the time.

In the end it is not my feelings that matter, but faith, faith that God is near no matter how I feel. As Saint Paul says, there remain faith, hope and love, and the greatest of these is love. Love flows from faith and hope and not from my feelings. Faith, hope and love: a little trinity that makes me one and makes God near.

HOW DO WE PRAY WITHOUT DETACHMENT, AND HOW DO WE TRY TO be detached without knowing what it is we're to be detached from? We begin to pray well as soon as we realize that complete detachment is never an accomplished fact. It is never realized completely, nor perhaps should it be. But in the process of trying to be reasonably detached, we pray. And prayer becomes more intense the more aware we are of our entanglements with things and people that distract us from God. This is not to say that things and people are not good. They are. But something has happened somewhere along the line; call it original sin or anything you like. The fact remains that most of our heartaches come from exaggerated attachments. And our peace flows from a love that does not so attach itself that it suffocates the beloved and the lover, as well.

It sounds old-fashioned to use words like "detachment," but our experience tells us daily that we are not really free and that there must be someone to love who transcends the *need* to be loved, a lover who invites rather than demands our love.

FOR YEARS NOW I HAVE BEEN RETURNING TO THIS SLATE GRAY TREE that winters outside my window. Years! And I realize that I don't even know for sure what kind of tree it is. I think it is a maple. But I do know the tree. Isn't it that way with so many of our experiences? We can't label them, and yet we know them as part of our daily experience.

Prayer is like that. People are always telling me that they would love to learn to pray. And then when I ask them how they pray now, they realize in telling me about it, that they have been praying for years. And I realize that they have been praying well. The reason they didn't think they were praying is that somewhere along the line they got it into their heads that prayer is some special, esoteric practice reserved for monks and nuns and mystics and has nothing to do with the lives of ordinary men and women. Nothing could be further from the truth. To pray is the privilege of every child of God. To speak to God is the gift of the Incarnation. Jesus has made it possible for us to cry out, "Abba, Father."

Furthermore, the Gospels tell us over and over again that God hears, that God listens to what we say; and even more wonderful, that God answers. But that short statement, "God answers," is where many of us begin to doubt. "If God answers," we say, "why doesn't God answer *me,* now, when I need it, when I'm begging for just one word from God's lips?" When I am filled with these kinds of doubts, I realize that one of two things has happened inside me: Either I am not listening as I could, or I am listening only for what I want to hear from God.

The first problem is a difficult one to overcome because it means that I have to learn all over again how to be still and quiet inside, to rest in God. And the second problem is even more difficult. If I am listening for only what I want to hear, then I have become selfish again, and I am listening only to myself. My prayer has turned into a monologue.

> I WRITE
> And you leap onto the page, O Lord.
> When I cannot write
> Will you leap back into my heart?

inner sounds

I GET WEARY OF TAKING PEN IN HAND AND TRYING TO THINK ON paper late at night. But always I remember that someone who is alone or afraid or just bored with life might someday read some small passage from these notes and take new courage or feel less alone or want to start living again. And perhaps that's why we pray when we are tired. Perhaps there is someone somewhere who needs our voice because his or hers sticks in the throat, or they have given up praying altogether. And we cannot sleep until we pray in their stead. Each of us is capable of being an instrument for another's cry or another's song. We join with Christ in redeeming our brothers and sisters. We cannot redeem them, but we have it in our power to effect some small change because we are joined to Christ, their Redeemer and Lord. We do make a difference for good or bad in all our brothers and sisters.

IN COMMUNION
    With these woods again,
  These trees waiting always
      At the edge of the property,
  The border of my solitude.

LATE AT NIGHT WHEN ALL THE SOUNDS OUTSIDE ARE QUIET, THE inner sounds sometimes clamor to be heard, and we toss and turn trying to still their demands. It is always the same: They win for a while and finally sleep comes—too late to bring that needed healing of mind and body.

> I REACH out to you, O Lord,
> And all I touch is my own emptiness,
> Air and silence and the memory
> That this kind of prayer never works for me.
> When I am most in need,
> Prayer never seems to help.
> It only strengthens my own helplessness.
> In your own way, in your own time
> You will answer. That I know, that
> I remember. So once again I lean on
> Patience. I wait. As before, there is
> This waiting, this dread that I
> Won't hold out. But I do, and
> That is perhaps your answer.
> We cannot stamp our feet or cry
> And expect you to come running.
> We only say, "Into your hands, O Lord."
> And there is peace, for you are faithful
> If not prompt, and you will answer
> When you will answer. Amen.

GOD IS LOVE. THAT IS ALL WE KNOW AND ALL THAT MATTERS IN THE end. For to say, "God is love," means that we are loved, and therefore we can love. Loving is all we can do that matters now or ever, and that is possible only because God is love. To love is to be, for

God *is* love. When we love, we *are*, for God is because God loves. I don't know if I understand this, but it consoles me.

I NEVER SEEM TO THANK YOU, GOD, AS EARNESTLY AS I ENTREAT YOU. Yet somehow I know that thanking you is much of what prayer is about. You are so good and so faithful and that alone should make my whole life an act of thanksgiving. And when on top of that, I call to mind all that you have done in my life, the countless attentions, the growing within me, the obstacles you have removed, the gift of your presence, I blush at my ingratitude and indifference at times. Like the sparrows that have always been in my life, you are so present that I take you for granted. And therefore I thank you now in the Eucharist, that perfect act of thanksgiving in which you give thanks for me, even when at Mass my mind and heart are elsewhere.

IN THE CRISES AND SORROWS OF OUR LIVES ONE OF THE FIRST questions we ask is, will someone be there, will anyone help to support us? In my own life this has become almost *the* definition of God: the One who is there. Not just in crises, of course, but always. And yet it is most difficult to believe that God is there if there is not another human being there as well. Perhaps it is the weakness of my faith, but it is so hard to believe that God is here with me if there is no one else besides. When others stand with us and beside us, God shines forth in our midst. So maybe God keeps coming to us in the form of those "angels" who look like human beings.

ONE DAY IS MUCH LIKE ANOTHER IN THE SEARCH FOR GOD. BUT from time to time there is a sudden, unexpected revelation, or shining forth of God. You're startled that you realize God is everywhere, in everything and everyone. Call it insight, epiphany, baptism in the spirit, or any other name, it is the same experience: The God within you is revealed fleetingly, and all the rest of your days are changed permanently. Something happens that you did not merit and that you cannot explain or communicate. But it is more real than any communicable experience, and you cannot formulate it or capture it in words; for to do so would be to have some hold on God, who cannot be captured in a phrase or formula. Nor can you, by remembering it, recapture the experience. It is gift; it is grace. The spirit blows where it will.

the silence inside

THE SILENCE OF GOD. IT IS SO DEAFENING THAT IF YOU ARE looking for a voice like any human voice that you can hear, you will surely give up on prayer and finally on God. God has spoken through the Scriptures and once for all through Jesus Christ, his Son. And that is all in the past. Or is it?

One of the surest effects of prayer is the conviction that God speaks to me here and now. God's voice is not something I hear with my human ear, but something inside me that vibrates to the word of God spoken in utter silence at the core of my being. God's voice is not a constant sound, but a presence that resonates somewhere deep within. And that felt resonance, like the mere touch of someone we love, is sufficient to keep us going months on end.

In saying that this experience is *felt* resonance, I do not mean to imply that the experience of God is necessarily an emotional experience felt along the heart. It is more often than not a deep conviction that something has happened or is happening to me that can be explained only by some divine epiphany, some shining forth, or revelation of the God who is always within me and who lets me experience that presence from time to time.

It is futile then to wait and listen for a voice from heaven to ring in the ear with some answer. The answer dwells within us, and now and then, it is uncovered and we know inexplicably that God is there.

"Credo ut experiar." "I believe in order that I may experience."

—Saint Bernard

To most moderns "detachment" is a medieval, dehumanizing word that separates us from the goodness and beauty of creation. It means separation and alienation from the nitty-gritty world. But that is not what spiritual detachment means. Like so much of the Christian mystery, detachment paradoxically means total involvement with life as we ordinarily understand that term. In order to be totally involved with you, I must somehow be detached from dependence on you; and if I am detached, you will not be enslaved by my involvement with you. It is as simple in essence, and as difficult to achieve, as that. And no one understands this perfect freedom and total involvement but him or her who has been loved by a saint. So once again the proof of words is verified in experience; without experience words are unconvincing, divisive and problematical.

God has called each of us to a special service of love and sharing. Most of the time that service is rendered in our ordinary, everyday living, but somehow we fail to see this fact and are constantly looking elsewhere to find ourselves. We think that our real call from God, our real identity, is just around the next corner, that surely God has something other in mind for us than the commonplace demands of our own families and friends, of our own neighborhood, our own town. And because of this attitude, we miss the real opportunities to discover who we really are, and we fail to grow to the stature in Christ that God intends for us. Jesus grew to manhood and holiness in the carpenter shop at Nazareth learning to live with and to love his parents, relatives and neighbors. We grow in love and holiness in the same way.

LORD, YOU draw me out.
You are more insistent
Than I want to believe
And so I fail to see my
Troubles as your probing,
Your way of saying that
I need to grow. I am
So blind to you that I
Pray for deliverance
From what you send
To make me whole.
Give me light to see by.

the people outside

GOD CARES. THAT IS SUFFICIENT. IT LASTS. BUT IN THE HUMAN condition there is more that we need: We need to know that God cares because other people care. In other words we are not isolated entities who relate exclusively to God. We are the Body of Christ, we are brothers and sisters in the Spirit; and that awareness makes tangible union with *the* other, who is God.

No other reality makes so powerful an impression on me as the fact that I am a member of the Body of Christ. That I am not alone, that I am joined inextricably with all Christ's members, makes God's caring something more than words. In Christ's Body I find his spirit, and in his members I discover who he is. This alone keeps the spiritual life from becoming ethereal and egocentric. For that spirituality which narrows down to God and myself actually zeroes in on myself in the end, and God becomes what I make God out to be. The communion of saints saves me from union with myself. God is revealed in incarnation, in enfleshment in all the members of Christ's Body that I relate to, whether I realize it or not.

The word was made flesh and dwelt, dwells and will dwell among *us*.

THE THINGS AND PEOPLE WE CLING TO IMPRISON US; THE THINGS and people we love free us. The most liberating experience of all is to love something or someone and not at the same time want to control the object of our love. True love allows the other his or her own freedom; yes, even desires that freedom; and in return the lover is free to love more and more selflessly.

Who, however, can achieve such love? Maybe no one can completely. But each one of us glimpses from time to time the exquisite joy of his or her selflessness. If I am willing to love you and let you go whenever and wherever you wish, we are both free and our love grows. Otherwise, need and dependence replace love, and we grow tired of what all of this is costing us emotionally.

Some learn this basic fact of life, and they become the saints we all know. Others never do learn it, and they are constantly caught in webs of their own making, unable to break loose and enjoy the freedom of the children of God.

WHAT IS THE PRICE OF LOVE? IS IT NOT TURNING LOOSE AND letting go of what we think we cannot live without? That letting go, paradoxically, binds the beloved to us, whereas the refusal to let go guarantees an early demise of love and the eventual loss of the beloved, and in the end, of ourselves. Somewhere in this simple truth of human relationships lies the mystery of the cross and of the Resurrection. Or perhaps it is our own experience of love that makes the cross and Resurrection of Christ believable.

SOMETIMES WE FEEL THAT GOD SHOULD BE MORE PRESENT TO US, more real, if for no other reason because of all the time and effort we have expended in trying to pray. But God, the exquisitely coy lover, never lets prayer become an end in itself or a vehicle by which we can capture or pin God down. There is no magic formula, no ritual that guarantees an instant God-experience. Every experience of God is a gift; God will not be tangibly present on demand.

What all this amounts to is that God is God and God's will is God's will. On the other hand God has told us through Jesus that anything we pray for in Jesus' name will be given us, and that we should pray always and never lose heart. And so we continue to pray in faith and wonder why God doesn't come and satisfy our longing. The only solution that satisfies me is that God is a lover and as such intensifies our longing and love by the lover's coyness. God draws near only to withdraw when we think we finally have God near us. Faith then replaces emotional experience with a new kind of experience, more real and more permanent than any transient feeling God might give us from time to time. Like real love faith endures when falling in love is over.

> WHEN THE wind returns
> The skies clear
> And my heart yearns
> To follow the wind.

HOW DO I KNOW MY PRAYER IS AUTHENTIC AND SINCERE? The age-old question. And today as always there is only one answer, and it is not in the prayer itself, but in what happens outside of prayer. Anyone can be "turned on" in prayer from time to time. But only the authentic person of prayer can be charitable. Again it is love that is the measure of anything in the life of the spirit. If I love God, I will keep his two great commandments, and no one will be deceived about whether I do or not. Either I am charitable or I am not. I cannot fake it the way I can fake prayer or piety.

Therefore I should not worry about my prayer. That will only turn me self-consciously inward, make me selfish and self-preoccupied. I need to worry about charity. Nothing takes me out of myself like trying to love my "enemy," nor is anything more impossible without God than true charity.

The measure of God's love for me is the gifts I receive in prayer, and certainly, the measure of my love for God is how charitable I am to my neighbor; and that is *the* gift of prayer. God's love for me in prayer is authenticated by my love for God in my neighbor.

prayer and play

PLAYFULNESS BEFORE GOD. EACH ONE OF US HAS TO BE SOMETHING of a fool, something of a court jester before God if we are not to take ourselves too seriously. And paradoxically, the more seriously we take God, the less seriously do we take ourselves. If I center in on God and make God the focus of my life, I gain perspective on myself and can laugh at my own seriousness, my own needless worries. God is within me, but God is also apart from me and draws me out of myself. Therefore any prayer that drives me inward and makes me self-conscious is not really prayer but introspection.

Unhealthy introspection that sometimes passes for prayer is what makes many sensible people shy away from "prayer." They just can't take too much soul-searching and navel-gazing. Prayer is not self-analysis but self-liberation through concentration on and absorption in God. Most of us need to forget ourselves if we are ever going to find ourselves. Ironically, however, we moderns seem always to be trying to find ourselves and we end up like the dog trying to chase its own tail: We spin around in endless circles. And the whole business is taken very seriously.

What we need is some humor, some playfulness. In order to play, I have to forget myself; the game has to absorb my attention so fully that I forget how I am feeling or who is watching me or how well I am playing. And it is better to play a little every day than to play for protracted periods on the weekend. So with prayer; a little self-forgetfulness and meditation every day goes a long way. Praying and playing are somehow a part of the identical experience just as foolishness and wisdom unite in the court jester. The prayer and the jester don't self-consciously look over their shoulders to see who is watching.

AT TIMES REACHING OUT FOR GOD CAN BE SOMETHING LIKE searching for your own identity: It is futile and self-defeating. In both cases it is better to reach out to other people and serve their needs. In so doing you will find God if you are seeking God, and you will find yourself as well. Those who are forgetful of themselves are inevitably the ones we most admire and love. They are in possession of themselves and we know it. And yet we perversely seek for God where we are least ourselves, in our own self-centeredness.

> PRAISE GOD for ever-caring,
> For being there when we
> Thought God was far away.
> God is faithful and all time
> Proves as much if we
> Are patient enough to wait
> For God's past faithfulness
> To register in our present
> Consciousness. Awareness
> Is the past catching up
> With the present and
> Disproving all our doubt.

WINTER

gray days

THE GRAY AND WET OF WINTER SOMETIMES SEEPS INTO THE SOUL and we pray for snow and ice to break the monotony of slate-colored days. Our life in God is like those gray days from time to time. Everything seems soggy and bogged down with water, and we feel heavy of heart. Wet days of the soul are for reaching out to others and not for meditating. Our inner weather is changed only by action, by charity, by breaking out of inward-looking melancholy. Yet so often we erroneously think that we must withdraw and think about our heavy mood and why it is upon us. Seldom, if ever, do we *think* ourselves out of occasional melancholy. Rather we *act* ourselves out of it by taking other peoples' needs more seriously than we take our own. We don't change the weather outside by wishing it away; we ignore it and go about our work. Inner weather is handled much the same way.

THERE'S SOMETHING ABOUT SNOW ON THE LANDSCAPE, SOMETHING clean and protective that insulates the heart and makes you feel secure. You don't notice the cold because usually you are inside a house or car looking out. And in a world of snow quiet subtly seeps into the heart.

The atmosphere for prayer is something like this experience. There must be silence outside, and the outside world must be some-how removed for the time of your watching. You then see your world from a new perspective. And even if it is cold and barren, you view it from the inner warmth of your own heart in union with God, and it looks white and beautiful again. Then you are ready to walk into the white snow made beautiful and warm by your new vision.

I WRITE THIS SENTENCE ONLY BECAUSE I PROMISED MYSELF I'D TRY to write at least one sentence every day, and because one sentence leads to another. If only we could pray a little every day, even when it is only one word; for prayers, like sentences, lead into more prayers, and eventually the heart hears and is lifted beyond the words to God who transcends all thought and every word.

THE WORLD IS WET WITH WINTER AS ASH WEDNESDAY DRAWS NEAR. The heaviness of water and the lightness of ashes mingle somehow in the soul seeking repentance. We are heavy with sins and attachments and long for that light touch of ashes that reminds us of the transitory nature of everyone and everything but God.

THESE SCATTERED THOUGHTS SHOULD NOT BE A REFLECTION *ON* but a reflection from within, the sparrow within me talking, trying to sing.

WHAT A TERRIFYING EXPERIENCE IS THE FEELING THAT YOU HAVE somehow been abandoned by God, that all your prayers have come to nothing, that perhaps there has been no one there all along and what you took for a relationship with God was in fact only yourself talking to yourself. Sooner or later this experience comes to everyone who tries to love God and to live a life of prayer. There is no way to prepare for it adequately or to avoid it, for it is God who calls you to this desert experience.

The only consolation when this barrenness is upon you is that it will pass, even though at the time the only thing you seem sure of is that it will not pass. And the only remedy is to turn determinedly to the service of others! The last thing in the world you feel inclined to do. What you want to do is withdraw into yourself and clamor at God's door begging for entrance. But if you leave that door and serve your brother and sister with all your heart, when you return, it will be standing open.

This service of others does not mean that you abandon prayer. Heaven forbid! It merely means that you try concentrating more on others than on yourself while continuing to pray in emptiness of spirit, not expecting any consolation or encouragement in return. And if you persevere in this routine (and it will seem terribly routine), God will return to you and lead you back to the open door and welcome you inside.

MY FIRST APRIL AFTERNOONS IN ASSISI. IT ALWAYS SEEMED TO BE raining, and the shuttered afternoon siestas were dark with sleep and black clouds that settled permanently on Mount Subasio. For me this insulating effect was never one of melancholy. Rather I felt somehow protected and warm with my thoughts, despite the chill that seeped through thick rock walls into the little corner room where I wrote and prayed and stared out the French windows at the fortress, the Rocca Maggiore, with its somber background of rain clouds. Perhaps I was so amazed and so thrilled to be in Assisi at all, that my inner weather counteracted and transformed anything negative that tried to invade it from without.

Many times since those first idyllic three months in Assisi, I have traveled there again in memory, and what was past becomes present again, even embellished by imagination's coloring of those graced days of 1972. I think this kind of experience speaks a great deal to us about what prayer is at times. Without our expecting it, our inner weather is suddenly all sunshine and light; and all those outer things that previously affected our moods so drastically seem unable to touch our inner peace and well-being. But like a European jaunt or a long-awaited vacation, these periods never last long. They are graces, gifts to be relished, to be gratefully enjoyed, even though we know rain clouds will eventually sift into our souls and settle down for awhile. But while the clouds are there, we have memory to keep us going.

l i s t e n i n g

THE ART OF LISTENING. HOW HARD IT IS TO CULTIVATE. WE SEEM TO be able to listen to others only so long before we start talking ourselves, usually about ourselves. It is that way with prayer, too. The hardest part is the listening, the quiet, the patience it takes to be still and wait upon God. We always want to start talking, and yet what more can we say beyond the words Christ gave us in the "Our Father"? If we spent time in prayer saying the "Our Father" once and then listening for the remainder of the time we set aside for prayer, it would be one of the best disciplines possible in learning to pray. But we are uncomfortable with silence, with waiting for the other to speak. This is strange, really, because we all know how much more is communicated in silent communion with someone we love than in a plethora of words that soon seem empty and repetitious. God, like all lovers, speaks louder in silence than in words spoken in a rush of emotion. And God hears us better in our silent awareness and concentration than in a multiplicity of words.

There are times, of course, when we pray in a rush of words and emotion, in times of great trouble or joy, for instance. But that is more for our sake than God's, who knows what we are going to say before we say it. The saying it, however, helps us and heals us in the release of pent up sorrow or lifts us up in the release of too much joy or gratitude. Generally, however, lovers speak in silence and hear in silence, and words only complicate the purity of their communion.

PRAYER IS NOT ONLY A NEED THAT EACH OF US HAS; IT IS ALSO A power. Jesus has told us that whatever we ask in his name, God will give us. And because prayer is a power, it is also a responsibility and challenge. It is a responsibility because through prayer we can join with Christ in redeeming the world. If we pray only for ourselves or about ourselves, we have not yet learned to pray, for prayer is out-ward-reaching and all-embracing. A good barometer of where we are in our union with God is whether or not our prayer reaches out to all people. If my prayer centers mainly on myself, then that is where I am. The true prayer accepts Christ's challenge to join with him in opening his or her arms to all. And as one's prayer becomes more cosmic and other-centered, so does one's thinking and attitudes.

I ONCE HEARD THE PHILOSOPHER GABRIEL MARCEL SAY, "I FOUND God in another person in whom God dwelt." I remember how stunned I was to hear this complex, deep man say something so sim-ple. I had expected some profound answer about his search for God through the circuitous route of his own existential thought. Instead, a simple statement and this in answer to a question from the audi-ence after a penetrating lecture on the theater of the absurd. A young man rose in the audience and asked Professor Marcel how he had found God, and in contrast to the complexity of his lecture, he said that he had found God in another person; it was as simple as that. This answer was something anyone could understand.

We are all, whether we realize it or not, living symbols of the presence of God in the world. By who we are and how we act we can either build up or tear down the kingdom of God. God has chosen to act through us humans, first through God's son, Jesus Christ, and then through all the members of Christ's Mystical Body. That God is alive and well is most evident in those who live through, with and in God. No greater compliment could be given a man or a woman than that someone should say, "I found God in you."

WHEN WE FINALLY COME TO LOVE OURSELVES, SOMETHING HAPPENS inside us that makes humility possible. I cannot humble myself if I think myself worthless or unworthy of love. It is only when I recognize that I am worthy and lovable that I can even *think* of humbling myself. If we try to humble ourselves before we love ourselves, we only sink more deeply into depression and low self-esteem. What most of us need is to know we are loved, to know we are worthwhile. And that is precisely what God wants to do for us.

WE PRAY AND WORRY, WORRY AND PRAY OVER SOME HEAVY BURDEN of mind or body, and nothing happens. Time passes. And all our hope rides away with time. Then, just when time's last car is passing by, with all our hope inside, the burden is lifted just in time for us to run lightly again and catch the last car. Why God lets us wait for that final car is a mystery, but perhaps that is what faith and hope are about—waiting. No instant answer, no instant changes. No ride on the first seat of the first car in a train, but just making the last car of a moving train with one seat left. Waiting and watching all those cars go by, too heavy to jump aboard, makes every ride a miracle and every leap something only God can accomplish in us.

> YOU, O Lord, are the one
> Who calls my name.
> I hear you in the place
> Called prayer, where
> Names are necessary
> Only in the beginning.

PRAYER LETS YOU EXPERIENCE THE GOSPEL PARADOX OF LOSING yourself in order to find yourself. The more you lose yourself in contemplation of God, the more yourself you become. You come away from prayer more convinced that you are someone special, having just talked with God. You know your name, and it sounds good to the ear. How this happens is a mystery, but it has its counterpart in human love. When I lose myself in someone I love, I feel more free, more independent than when I am alone; and I am full, not empty, when I give myself away.

SIMPLICITY OF STYLE. IN ART AS IN LIFE SIMPLICITY HAS ITS OWN charm. The simple word is often the exact word that triggers complex responses within us. The simple person, we feel, has somehow passed through complexity and confusion, and his or her simplicity is really transcendence and victory over the inessential entrapments of life.

In prayer we learn the simple word that effects and flows from a simple life. Our life and prayer are so intertwined that they too, become a new simplicity of word and act. There is a Chinese proverb on the wall of the children's museum in Boston that sums up simply what I am trying to say so falteringly:

> I hear…and I forget.
> I see…and I remember.
> I do…and I understand.

Very simply, that is prayer and action integrated.

WE STRAIN HARD AT TIMES, LISTENING FOR THAT ONE WORD, THAT voice of assurance from the other side. And when the strain becomes too much for us, we go back to feverish activity and diversion convinced that prayer is not for us, that it is a gift God gives to special souls. Then something draws us back again, some hope that this time it will work. What draws us back is something inside us, something that was there from the beginning. And that movement from within, that drive is really the voice of God that we were listening for "out there" somewhere. In other words, more often than not, the "voice of God" is a force within us propelling us toward God. It is God leading us.

But we remain frustrated because we are never satisfied with what happens at that rendezvous called prayer. If there *is* satisfaction of any kind, it is so short-lived that we wonder if it was worth it. And yet we return to prayer again and again. And in the returning we notice something happening, not during prayer exactly, and not all of a sudden. But gradually something has been happening to us. *We* are changing. A peace and calm is settling into our lives and we begin to hear God's Word in Scripture in a way we didn't before. It is somehow more personal, more directly related to our lives. The Mass takes on a new meaning, and we yearn for frequent union with Christ in the Eucharist.

In brief, what we had been expecting to happen suddenly in prayer, had been happening gradually in our daily lives.

open spaces

SOMETIMES THE REASON WE CANNOT PRAY IS THAT WE HAVEN'T ANY space left in our lives. We are psychologically, spiritually, and perhaps even physically hemmed in. We are moving at such a frenetic pace and the press of responsibilities and the people who make inroads on our time and energy is so great that we really haven't any space left for ourselves. If we try then to use the little time we have left for prayer, we come to prayer already exhausted and tense.

It would be better, if such is our situation, to take some positive steps to reduce the pressures in our lives and provide some extra space for leisure and relaxation. And certainly before trying to pray at the end of the day it is better to unwind first from the pressures and tensions of work. In providing space and relaxation we are making remote preparations for the calm and tranquility necessary for listening to God.

Prayer and life are so intimately intertwined that we must be sensible in both areas if we are to achieve the kind of integration that God intends for us. Most of us so overextend ourselves in work and attending to the needs of others, that we leave little to God or for God. We need to put our lives and the worry about them more and more into God's hands and spend more time with God in prayer. The result will be an increased alertness and ability to do our daily tasks with energy and enthusiasm and a growing awareness of God's care and providence in our daily lives.

DOES ANYTHING HAPPEN IN PRAYER THAT IS NOT JUST THE RESULT OF relaxation and a kind of self-hypnosis? Is there in fact a real contact with God? And if there is, how do we know it? These are questions I have never been able to answer to my own satisfaction, and yet I know that something does happen in prayer. At least I know that God hears and answers my prayer. But that I have ever heard God, I don't know. I do know that from time to time God's Word in Scripture is sweet to my heart and I feel that God is reaching into the very center of me. And at the beginning of my journey to God I felt God's presence everywhere. But how much of that sweetness and consolation was God and how much was my own enthusiasm is hard to say.

Ultimately what I *can* say is that I know God most when God withdraws, when I no longer feel anything. It is something God does without warning, and then I know that God was certainly there because of the emptiness and panic of God's leaving. And then I understand that for me God's presence is most heard or seen in its removal. Then I know that loneliness which makes for hell.

In saying God is known only in God's leaving, I am making an extreme statement which must be qualified. There are from time to time, but very rarely, deep and very real "experiences" of God. These visitations are untranslatable, but they are attested to by many spiritual writers and mystics. Usually, these experiences come early, if not at the very beginning, of one's conversion to the interior life, and the memory of them sustains us for years. But they are by no means the staple of the spiritual life. Our life in God is nourished primarily by word and sacrament and not by felt religious experience. This is why I make the seemingly extravagant statement that God is known experientially only in God's leaving. And I am speaking, of course, of ordinary men and women and not of special people like Moses whom "the Lord knew fact to face" (Deuteronomy 34:10).

LATE AT NIGHT WHEN I STRUGGLE TO PEN A FEW WORDS ON PRAYER, I realize how little I know about prayer. And that is perhaps why I continue to try to write about it. I feel that if I try writing about it often enough, it may come clear to me. I'm probably deluding myself and should be spending these late evening hours praying instead of writing about prayer. Or do I pray with pen in hand? Maybe that is the trouble; I'm writing letters to God instead of talking to God. But that seems how I best communicate with God at times, because writing leads into real prayer, just as writing to a loved one brings him or her to mind, and the person becomes present as we write and see in the mind's eye the one we're writing to. Writing for me is remote preparation for prayer. Each person finds his or her own avenue to God in that which prepares the heart to listen and speak to God.

FOR YEARS NOW I HAVE USED A LITTLE MEMORY DEVICE TO HELP people who are learning to pray. The memory help is the word SPORT, each letter of which stands for a different step in prayer.

The S stands for silence, probably one of the most difficult parts of prayer. In order to pray well, we must become interiorly silent; we must let all our tensions and preoccupations drain away and let a calm and soothing spirit descend upon us. Just trying to achieve this quiet of mind and heart might take up most of our prayer time, but it is necessary to all that follows.

The P stands for purification. If I am going to pray well, I must be able to purify my heart, and that means I must be able to forgive. I must try, at least, to forgive all the hurts I have received in my life. I must even try to forgive myself as God forgives me. If I cannot forgive someone, then my prayer remains on that level, and it does not deepen and grow until I can forgive.

The O stands for openness. Once I am interiorly still and have forgiven or tried to forgive my neighbor from my heart, then I am ready to be open to God's Word. I can open the Scriptures and read what God's Word is saying to me, or I can just remain silent and let God speak in the depths of my heart.

The *R* stands for response. What does God want me to do? What is God saying to me now and how am I going to respond? All prayer leads somehow into concrete action, for prayer and life are one act of love.

The *T* stands for talking. Only now am I ready to talk to God. Notice that up till this time I have been quiet; I have been listening, open to God. The *T* could also stand for thanksgiving, letting thanks rise to my lips for all the Lord has done for me, especially in this brief period of prayer that God has granted me. And finally, the *T* could stand for time. None of this is possible without taking time to do it. Prayer requires unhurried time to just be in the presence of God.

This is one simple way of praying. It is not the only way, but it is a beginning. God will bring it to perfection.

THERE IS AN OLD SAYING THAT GOD CAN WRITE STRAIGHT WITH crooked lines. How often each of us has experienced something like that in his or her life!

I WRITE, NOT BECAUSE I KNOW, BUT BECAUSE I DON'T KNOW. Similarly, I pray, not because I know how to pray, but because I don't. This is not false humility but the truth. Those who wait until they know, will never write, and those who sit back and wait for the gift of prayer, some grand inspiration, will pray very little, if at all. The prayer is a searcher who reaches out for God, most of the time clumsily and without satisfaction. And through all of this he or she is praying in the Spirit.

The reason I make this last statement is that some falsely believe that they are praying in the Spirit only when they are filled with joy and enthusiasm and when they tangibly experience the influx of the Spirit and break into spontaneous praise and thanksgiving. But that is only one form of praying in the Spirit, for life is not a continuous celebration. It is rather a rhythm of joys and sorrows, certitude and doubt, fullness and emptiness, intimacy and loneliness, turning inward and turning outward. And our prayer reflects this same rhythm as did the prayer of Jesus.

But one thing is certain: When we pray, no matter how we are feeling, the Spirit prays with us and within us with "unutterable groanings."

running

EVERY ONCE IN A WHILE A PERSON WHO IS TRYING TO PRAY IS tempted to leave everything and go away into some wilderness to be alone with God. He or she thinks, "Yes, there I could really pray; there my prayer would soar to heaven on wings."

We would all like to withdraw from life awhile, and from time to time it is good to retreat with God; but our prayer is best and most sincere when we pray wherever we are.

Prayer that rises spontaneously from our everyday lives is our real prayer, the real gauge of how earnestly we are trying to live in and for God. What I do and how I act from day to day is more indicative of who I am than the extraordinary things I do, and how I pray from day to day says more about my interior life than infrequent spurts of devotion or a period here and there of intense prayer and meditation.

SOMEONE, A LOVELY LADY AND POET, SENT ME A COLLECTION OF Italian poems. This one I love. It is called *"E tu Iddio,"* "You, God." The poet, Danilo Dolce; the poem written in 1924; the translation:

YOU, GOD
You, God
Because of whom I walk in this boundless sky
among clouds of worlds

You are lonelier, poorer than I;
I have seen you wince under the surgeon's
scalpel removing an ulcer from your bowels.
I have seen You dead drunk
staggering empty-eyed,
I have seen You
tense pushing a laden wheel-barrow,
jump for joy over new pockets
over shiny shoes
and call out to me, and stretch out Your hands
happy over a smile and a little kiss.
Those sparrow-like eyes of yours
make me sad.
In order to live, I must be a brother
and a father to You.
And wipe your running nose
and support you in your faltering steps,
build you a stout house
of solid stone in fine plumb, and heal you
if your head limply resting on my knees
burns with fever,
and fetch you bread, soup
and honey and the fruit you like:
it is my way of adoring you.

LATELY I FIND MYSELF THINKING MORE ABOUT PRAYER AND PRAYING less. A lot of us are like that; instead of doing, we think. We do this because in thinking, we can remain locked up in ourselves; but to actually pray, we have to break out and lift our minds and hearts to God. We have to try to communicate and listen to the other, and that is difficult. When we just think about prayer, it's like talking about writing, and not writing. We then don't know writing at all because we haven't experienced it in process but only as a finished product to be analyzed. Real prayers often don't know how to talk about prayer and don't really think about it that much; they pray, and that is sufficient.

If you don't pray, God is a name; if you do, God is a person.

LORD, I used to think
That you hid from me.
But lately I realize
More and more that
I'm the one to blame:
I don't play games well.
I keep missing you,
Keep being blind and
Bad at finding people
And things and you.

I KEEP writing
After midnight,
Hoping I might
Help you who bite
Your fingernails,
Sleepless, afraid.

letting god be god

IN GOD'S HANDS. HOW OFTEN WE SAY THAT AND WANT TO BE ABLE to believe it, but such surrender demands so much faith and trust in God. We would much prefer doing everything ourselves rather than putting things in God's hands. It seems hard enough just to stop working and worrying long enough to spend time with God in prayer, let alone having the trust to turn over our lives and let God "worry" for us.

Our life with God is an intimate relationship with a person, and it works much the same as the relationships we have with others. If we have to do everything ourselves and never trust anyone else, we find ourselves not only doing everything alone but after awhile we *are* very much alone. We have no friends, and it's hard to talk to people or listen to them. If, however, we work with others and let them share with us, we grow in an awareness of our essential communion with other people; and because we have shared responsibilities and play, sorrow and joy, we find it much easier to communicate verbally and nonverbally as well.

From this very human fact of our experience we learn something about our relationship with the most important Person of our lives. We have to let God share by trusting and letting God into the practical, day-to-day side of our lives. We have to let God act. And if we do, then our prayer takes on all kinds of new dimensions. We have a lot to talk to God about because God's been sharing the whole day with us. God has been there, so there are a lot of things we feel we don't have to say. We can be silent together in the day's failures and/or successes.

In order to reach this stage of prayer, however, we have to be able to put at least some things in God's hands and trust. How easy to say; how hard to do.

ONE WHO CAN PUT THINGS IN GOD'S HANDS AND TRUST GOD grows daily in the knowledge that for one who loves God, all things work together unto good. Out of the great sorrows and pain of one's life come goodness and beauty and insight one never had before. Someone, I think it was the novelist Leon Bloy, once said that there are places in the human heart which do not yet exist, and into the heart comes suffering that they may exist. Out of such a heart prayer rises naturally as thanksgiving for the wholeness of everything that is, as a hymn to God who draws good even out of what we thought was evil.

NO MATTER HOW MUCH I PRAY, I STILL END UP SAYING, MOST OF THE time, "Lord, teach me to pray." I suppose in one sense we never learn to pray, we never feel that we have arrived. If we did feel that way, we would stop praying, for we would possess what prayer yearns for, an experienced union with God. Our yearning and never really learning helps us to keep praying.

THOSE WHO CARRY THE SICK TO THE POOL OF BETHESDA. THAT IS the image that crosses my mind when I think of those saintly men and women whose daily prayers are mostly for others. They lift people up and carry them to the healing pool of Bethesda, to the living waters of Christ himself. There are so many who do not pray or do not know how to pray, and they lie helpless right next to the water that could give them new life. And we, by our prayers for them, bring them to that water.

WHY DO WE PRAY WHEN NO ANSWER SEEMS FORTHCOMING? IS IT because we hope against all odds that we will hear the answer we are expecting? Or is it because we have "heard" something before and hope against hope that we will hear it again? Both responses sound cynical, but both are true sometimes when we bite our lips and pretend that we are hearing and talking to God the way other people say they do.

Some of our anxieties about prayer come from what preachers, authors, and our acquaintances say they experience. It is usually quite different from the darkness that we walk in, from the emptiness we feel most of the time. Like so many other things in our lives, we're wise to trust our own experience, as poor and simple as it may seem at times. God comes to each one of us in God's own way and time, and in the manner best suited to each person. God doesn't come according to some manual or primer of prayer, but according to our need and readiness.

And so we keep praying, remembering how God came before and we try to ignore the self-proclaimed prayers who tell us there is something wrong with us, that we are putting some barrier in God's way. We keep praying because common sense tells us God is more loving and more aware of who we are and what we need than those advisers who are more like Job's accusers than those wise of spirit.

GOD LOVES US. IF ONLY WE COULD HOLD ON TO THAT ABOVE everything else. We long to believe it. We want above all else to profess it. We know it is true. But others sometimes make us doubt it because they seem not to care. And, of course, what we can see and hear and touch moves us more than what we believe. It is only when belief conquers negative experience that we are truly men and women of faith.

THE SEARCH FOR GOD ENDS UP IN THE END BEING GOD'S SEARCH for us. We take so many wrong turns just where we might have met God at some corner of our life. But in the end God surprises us by finding us looking in the wrong direction. God comes our way, no matter how far afield we are. God goes out of the way for us; that is the story of God. We are that important; that is our story.

GOD DOES NOT GIVE US GRACE FOR THE FUTURE, BUT FOR THE present because the future is not yet. I become more and more convinced of this: If I pray for something that is in the future, my worries seem only to increase. But if I pray and live each day as it comes, God gives me the grace to bear the burden of each particular day. I wonder if other people experience the same thing.

WINTER WOODS
Winter woods, when
Did you become so silent?

a bow in god's hands

THERE IS A POINT OF SURRENDER IN OUR LIVES THAT WE YEARN FOR and strive for but seldom reach. And that is to turn completely to God and let ourselves go, to be able to put everything in God's loving hands. This is the final stage of our relationship with God, a relationship which the Greek poet and novelist Nikos Kazantzakis put so succinctly in his autobiographical novel *Report to Greco*. The book begins with this epigraph:

> Three kinds of souls, three prayers:
> 1. I am a bow in your hands, Lord. Draw me, lest I rot.
> 2. Do not overdraw me, Lord, I shall break.
> 3. Overdraw me, Lord, and who cares if I break!

I don't think these are three kinds of souls necessarily; they are stages in our journey to God. We begin enthusiastically, then we become afraid, then we surrender; and in that surrender we return to our first enthusiasm again.

MOST OF THE TIME I FIND IT DIFFICULT TO PRAY SIMPLY BECAUSE I am too concerned with my own affairs. I insist on setting everything right all by myself. And I see the same fault in so many others. We form a large part of humankind, I'm afraid. If we "have to" do everything ourselves, we do not realize our fundamental dependence on God, and most of our activity is fruitless toil that exhausts us rather than fulfills us. God's will becomes secondary to our own.

We must, of course, work, but the attitude we bring to work makes all the difference. As Saint Francis admonished his friars, we must work so as not to extinguish the spirit of prayer and holy devotion to which all things must be subservient.

PEOPLE WERE ALWAYS EXPECTING JESUS TO BE SOMEONE OTHER THAN he was. They thrust their own image of the Messiah upon him and insisted that he be a king like other kings they knew. How much pain and frustration that must have caused him, knowing that he couldn't be what they wanted him to be. And the more he tried to be who he really was, the more they rejected him and misunderstood him.

We, too, experience this kind of suffering, because we seldom measure up to what others expect us to be. And, as in other experiences of our lives, we know that Jesus has been there before us. And that makes it somehow important that we keep trying to be ourselves.

SPRING

springtime
of the soul

ON CLEAR DAYS IN EARLY MARCH, WHEN THE WIND BLOWS ALL DAY long, everything seems cleaner, and it's easy to puff up your lungs and inhale spring. There are soul days like that, too. Something clicks inside and everything seems bright and clear again. Then joy and gratitude rise to the lips spontaneously, and it is easy to praise God for all the lightness you feel within. It is spring in your soul.

MARCH SNOW
An indignant robin
Ruffles her feathers
And broods darkly
Over Ohio weather
That surprised her
With snow on her
Comfortable perch.
Sparrows aren't so
Indignant to snow.

MARCH WIND
The wind is back.
Suddenly without warning
It blows through the mind.

Will it clear the clouds
Or only chill the air and
Bring a fresh pall of snow?

GOD IS AS CLOSE TO US AS WE ARE TO OURSELVES. WE REACH OUT TO God and go on pilgrimage and search for God in other people, and all along God is closer to us than anything or anyone or any place where we are trying to find God.

One reason we may not be able to find God in ourselves is that we are out of touch with our true selves. We are uncomfortable with who we are; and until we learn to love ourselves, the search for God wearies us and we are constantly being frustrated. The paradox in all of this is that we cannot set out deliberately to love ourselves in order to find God. We have to lose ourselves by giving up the search for God and for ourselves and direct our lives toward the poor, the sick, the prisoners, the hungry and the thirsty. That in itself sounds like insanity to anyone who hasn't experienced the futility of trying to find oneself and God any other way.

The other paradox is that we lose ourselves to find ourselves through others, but we need solitude to do that. We need to have human relationships, but we also need breathing space from others. There is a balance here somewhere which only the Spirit of God reveals to us once we let go a little and learn to hold ourselves and others more gently. If we hold on too tightly, we and others and God all slip through our fingers and become remote. God is as close to us as we are to ourselves and others. When we hold ourselves gently, it is easier for what we really want to follow.

BEACH
Bodies huddled together
on the beach
so far from one another's
reach.

HOW OFTEN in prayer we
keep coming back to ourselves,
our own worries and concerns,
and forgetting altogether the One
we're talking to and listening for.

being and doing

SOMETIMES WE FRITTER OUR LIVES AWAY WAITING FOR SOMETHING to happen from our prayer. We fret and worry and pray desperately when what we need to do is to make some decision, to make some move forward from our entrenched predicament. We need perhaps to reach out to someone other than God for help, guidance, or support. Prayer must initiate or continue some action in our lives or it degenerates into a security blanket of some kind that seems to justify our doing nothing but praying.

In other words, we are back to the old truism that prayer and action go together and we can't have one without the other.

> DECISION
> Now, Lord it is time.
> I will away from me
> Into you and your world.
> As much as I fear you,
> It is too much for me
> Here alone with myself.
>
> LORD,
> I don't have to pray to you
> Somewhere out there beyond

These scattered rain clouds
That threaten the beach with dark.
I'm talking to you right now,
Right here inside me. Clouds
Don't matter really, or anything
Else that is out there beyond me.

WRITING AGAIN.
That is important,
More important
Than sun and sea
And warm beaches:
They *are;* writing *does.*

THE JOURNEY INTO MYSELF IS THE MOST FRIGHTENING OF ALL adventures.

CAN ANYONE MAKE US CONSCIOUS OF GOD BUT GOD? CONSCIOUS in the sense of aware, perhaps; but consciousness that implies an experience of the living God, only God can effect in us.

FLY THE wind
Before the calm;
There will be time
For a healing balm
After the climb.

WALKING THE beach in the early sun
We suddenly lift our heads and run
Moved by some crazy impulse to speed.
What we really need, who knows?
It's what we do remembering the blows
We've suffered and still aren't freed.

WE FIGHT SURRENDER TO GOD AND RESIST IT. THEN ONE DAY WE WAKE up and realize that letting go is the only answer. And waking up is pretty much what happens. Everything before that insight was a sleeping away of our lives in fear and trepidation. Then we jump out of bed and start living fully for the first time. Nothing matters from then on but God's will, and God absorbs our failures and our successes, and we praise God no matter what happens.

THE KINGDOM OF HEAVEN IS WITHIN YOU. WHY THEN SHOULD YOU falter? Trust Christ who reigns inside you, surrender yourself to him and believe that he cares almost as much as you do about your life!

Whenever I write about how little we trust God, it helps me to see again how little *I* trust him. It is *I* who think I care more about me than God does, that I have to do everything so that someone in heaven will notice, maybe. And in truth Christ is here all along loving me and sharing everything with me. And not Christ alone but the whole kingdom of heaven is with me and for me. Why then should I ever lose heart? Turn inward in prayer—there is God and the kingdom.

> I STAND in the woods
> And weep for the wind
> That blew through my mind
> When woods were somewhere
> To go that mattered.
> Now I walk through them
> For exercise.

> WHERE HAVE all the words flown
> That came so easily to mind a short time ago? I search
> The skies for their winging back:
> Nothing there but blue-black.

prayer and madness

A man needs a little madness or else he never dares cut the rope and be free.

—Zorba

LORD, I pray for this
Freeing madness, this
Unbinding bond with you.
But I hold myself too tightly
For this ever to happen
Unless you take my arms
From clutching myself
And let them embrace others
Instead. I yearn for this
But keep my arms around
Myself tighter than ever.

From the play, *Zalmen, or the Madness of God,* by Elie Wiesel:

Inspector: And you, Rabbi? Which side are you on? The question or the answers?
Rabbi: I am on the side of prayer.
Inspector: What is prayer; question or answer?

Rabbi: Both. Question for whoever believes he has found an
answer. Answer for whoever struggles with the question.

IF WE WERE TO ATTAIN WHAT WE REACH FOR IN PRAYER, THEN PRAYER
would be unnecessary. We reach out to God in prayer, and usually
we are frustrated. Some books on prayer make me wonder if the
author isn't exaggerating his or her own experience or putting into
the book what the author would like his or her prayer life to be
rather than what it really is. An active prayer life does not mean an
ongoing experience of God. On the contrary, it usually means an
ongoing hunger for the God who seems not to be there. Like everything else worthwhile in the human condition, prayer is difficult and
seldom brings with it the comfort and fulfillment so many authors
say it is supposed to bring.

And still we continue to pray, just as we continue to love even
though love is not everything it is romanticized to be. The need to
pray, like the need to love, comes from deep within; and I suspect
more people pray than we know of. Not everyone has faith, of
course, but with or without faith, people pray or want to pray.

WHEN WE EMBARK ON THE JOURNEY OF PRAYER, WE ARE WISE TO
know from the beginning that we are in for all the disillusionment and
frustration that a long journey involves. We may not even persevere to
the end; but even if we do, the way will not be easy. It will, however, be
a challenge to and an adventure of the spirit. What this means in practical terms is that it takes a certain inner toughness to enter into prayer
and persevere in it.

GOD HEARS ME. WE WANT TO BELIEVE IT WITH ALL OUR HEARTS,
and so we pray mightily and storm heaven with our cries. And the
silence terrifies us. We turn inward to the God who dwells within
and there is only emptiness there. And yet we believe. We know God
is there because the mustard-seed faith we do have is stronger than

the mountain of doubt that threatens it. That is the only way I can explain how my little faith continues to win over the emptiness and doubt that seems so large, so terrifying. God hears me pray and beg for a strong, courageous faith, and God keeps sending mustard seeds, and they are sufficient. I suppose we always want more than we really need while God continues giving us our daily bread.

song of the
sparrow

THE SPARROWS are all gone.
Or so I thought. Actually
I forgot to look for them.
They're always there
Beyond the imprisoned self.
God is that way, too.
Only, God's inside the self
As well as out there.
So close yet so far
From the self turned in
Upon itself.

I pray to you, Lord,
Let me not forget
The sparrows, for they
Remind me that I
Am more to you
Than many sparrows
Who mean so much to me.

Behind everything
And within everything
Are you, O Lord.

And we do not
See and hear you
Except in those things
And persons you
Inhabit. Why then
Do we expect a word
From you directly?
Things and people
Should be sufficient,
But sadly they are not.

Dear Lord,
I want you
And only you;
But somehow
You want me
To have you
Only through
Others. Who
Am I to want
What you do not
Want for me?
This mystery
I will never
Understand:
That you want
To be known
Through others
And when we
Try to find you
Apart from them,
You are not there
For finding.

SPRING RAIN
Dark rain flooding
New green fields and trees,
Washing past the leaves into dark roots.
I watch the rain
And feel it washing me,
Running down my body
Into soil without roots
Of mine. My roots are
Inside where rain
Never enters. I pray
For inner rain, O Lord,
Don't send me
Sterile thunder.

THE MYSTIC CANNOT LIVE WITHOUT DIVINE NEARNESS. ITS ABSENCE
drives him or her to a sort of madness or to a human love which they
see as a betrayal, innocent though it may be.

FOR A NUN
Like your Hopi pottery bowl,
hollowed out, open, beautiful,
you're being hollowed out by God
not to be filled but to embrace
the sculpted space itself, empty
yet filled with what you almost see:
intimate poverty's body.

GOD'S LOVE, WHEN IT COMES TO US THROUGH OTHER PEOPLE, OVER-
WHELMS us so. The reason is, I think, that God is always more con-
vincing enfleshed, and that is what Incarnation is all about. The
Incarnation was not a once-upon-a-time event. It recurs each time we
find God in another human being. People like you and me *are* in fact
the Body of Christ.

darkness
and light

SOMETIMES PRAYER IS NOTHING MORE THAN THE SEARCH FOR THE proverbial "light at the end of the tunnel." We walk in darkness, groping and stumbling and not really believing there is a light or an end to the tunnel. At times like these we can do no more than continue stumbling and groping. In other words, we continue to pray, despite the darkness and the seeming hopelessness of it all. Only in this way do we reach the new light that God is holding out to us.

If we stop and give up, we remain in darkness until God drills through the earth and lights our way where we are. This light, however, is not the light that would have been ours had we continued walking the tunnel God prepared for us. And God becomes the great miracleworker who rescues us, not the lover who waits patiently at the end of the tunnel for our own love and devotion to bring us to God.

> LORD, LET me find you
> When I am alone
> And when I'm with others.
> Do not let my solitude
> Turn into loneliness,
> Or my communion
> With others become
> Separation from you.
> Alone or peopled

My heart puts you
In the center.

THE HEART that reaches out
For God, first *around others*
And then *through* them
To God who dwells inside
The people we love.
It is a journey fraught
With indirections
And the temptation is
To stop with the other
Who is not God.

JESUS RETURNS TO US THROUGH HIS HOLY SPIRIT. HE IS BORN IN US AND we manifest him to others as Mary did when she surrendered herself to the Holy Spirit and said, "Behold the handmaid of the Lord; be it done unto me according to thy word."

MARY IS *THE* HUMAN MODEL OF LOVE. BECAUSE OF HER SPECIAL relationship to the Holy Spirit, she, like Don Quixote in the song, *The Impossible Dream,* had to love others pure and chaste from afar, and this included her love for Joseph, her husband. This does not mean that she never touched Saint Joseph or held him, but that their married love never achieved the union that all married love seeks. The reason for this is not that there is something wrong with sexual love; it is because she was already married to the Holy Spirit. The Holy Spirit overshadowed Mary and she became the mother of God. Mary then becomes the model of all virginal love, of all celibate love. Because the virgin is wed to God, his or her love for others is not about sexual union. But again this does not mean that the virgin stops loving or keeps others at a "safe" distance. In fact because of the virginal person's deep love of God he or she can love others deeply and really.

a clearing
in the woods

THERE IS AN IMAGE FROM EARLY AMERICA THAT FLASHES ACROSS MY mind whenever I think of contemplation or meditation. It is an image of a pioneer hacking down trees, trying to make a small clearing in the wilderness, a clearing for living and planting, a place where things will grow. That is what one who prays must do, make out of the maze of daily living a small clearing where he or she can be at peace, where God can plant the seed of God's Word, where the prayer can watch things grow. It is a task as difficult as subduing the wilderness and it is never finished because the wilderness constantly creeps in again with weeds and undergrowth that threaten to choke out what was cultivated with so much care. But this clearing in the woods is necessary if one is ever to learn the art of prayer.

How this clearing is achieved is as individual as we are. And the woods themselves have a fascination that often prevents us from even wanting a clearing. As the poet Robert Frost says, "The woods are lovely, dark and deep."

I NEVER SEEM TO LEARN TO PRAY, LORD, SO I TAKE PEN IN HAND AND hope these few lines will help hold you. You are always near, but I somehow drift away, caught up in my own preoccupied self. I'm always preparing to meet something you would take care of for me if only I let you, if only I would trust you. I am your own poor instrument. Take me up in your presence and show me what to do, for I am so ignorant of what I should do, of what you want me to do; I look everywhere for signs of your will that fit my own. They never substitute for your own voice deep inside my heart.

NIGHT THOUGHTS
The way the wind sounded
In the trees last night
Reminded me again
Of other nights that now
In memory are full of light.

CONTEMPLATIVE PRAYER IS POSSIBLE ONLY WHERE THERE IS QUIET and where there is time that is unhurried. Quiet and time. Both are more internal than external. I must be quiet on the inside and the time I take out for prayer must be time for "wasting," time. This attitude of mind is not easy to acquire, for always there is something more important to do, or there is something gnawing away at my attention, and try as I may, I just can't become quiet inside. And yet if I continue trying to attain this kind of tranquility, it happens from time to time like a sweet gift from heaven, that I *am* caught up in the silence and timelessness of God.

PRAYER
"I love you"
Is too direct
But it is all.
You need me
To say it,
So I do.
On paper
It looks and
Sounds as cheap
As not saying it
Really is.

SUMMER

It's summer, over thirty years on and the sparrows are still here, and I am once again jotting down the way it's been and how it is now with God and us.

journeys

A SUMMER SUNDAY EVENING ON THE LAKE SHORE LIMITED FROM New York City to Cleveland. We are passing along the Hudson River at sunset, a red glow on the New Jersey hills across the river as we approach the tip of Manhattan.

I pray for loved ones as I watch the broad Hudson flat and smooth at this hour.

Like a hammered bronze shield the river reflects the reddening sky and turns silver as the glow of the setting sun gradually wanes and the gray light of twilight irons out the red tints on the water. We pass Dobs Ferry just as the sun pops up over a low hill for a few seconds, rouging the water as if for a festive celebration. Swiftly we pass Irvington—for Washington Irving? The crests of the hills across the Hudson burn as in an Irving tale. The clouds form fantastic shapes. Is Sleepy Hollow Cemetery near? I wonder; and just as I'm thinking these thoughts, we pass Tarrytown and, yes, I murmur, here is Ichabod Crane and Rip Van Winkle and the Headless Horseman.

Dark hills now, black with a hint of blue where the remaining twilight breaks through. *Idyllic* seems an understated word for the magic that light and shadow, red glow and bronzed river turning to silver, and the memory of reading Irving creates. I reach for color, but I have no art with paint and brush. I wish I could reach up to a shelf of Irving works and pull down what his words painted there of black hills and blue as we rush through Ossing, where mallards group like an escutcheon on the burnished shield of a Hudson inlet that will bring us into Croton-Harmon.

How is it I'm mesmerized here, so far from the New Mexico landscape of my youth? And why is this landscape so congenial, so familiar? Isn't it because it is already inside me in the words of Irving who made this landscape a part of my own interior geography through the enchanting power of words like these from *The Legend of Sleepy Hollow*?

> In the bosom of one of those spacious coves which indent the shore of the Hudson, at the broad expansion of the river denominated by the ancient Dutch navigators as the Tappan Zee, and where they always prudently shortened sail, and implored the protection of Saint Nicholas when they crossed, there lies a small market-town or rural port, which by some is called Greensburgh, but which is more generally and properly known by the name of Tarry Town. This name was given, we are told, in former days, by the good housewives of the adjacent country, from the inveterate propensity of their husbands to linger about the village tavern on market days.[1]

Once one has fallen under the spell of words like these, reading becomes a transporting inner journey of particular intensity. It's the way many of us as children began to enter the marvelous world of the imagination. Not that we remember verbatim words like these, but their echoes, their feel, are in us, as they were in me; and on returning home, I looked up the actual words and reread them,

---

1. Charles Nieder, ed. and intro., *The Complete Tales of Washington Irving*. (Garden City, N.Y.: Doubleday, 1975), p. 31.

imagining again and remembering how they were there in the way I saw the Hudson that summer Sunday evening on the train.

Words like those I've quoted here inspire me not only to think and see, but to write, as well. I am moved by them to make my own words, to push words around on the page in order to process with words my own inner and outer landscapes.

Many today keep a journal of their own inner life. They try to make sense of their day by finding words that say how they feel and what's happening or has happened to bring them to the writing page. But there is more to writing than just saying how you feel and what you think; for to know what you think and feel, it's often necessary to see what you see and to let the seeing and how you describe it show you what you think and what you feel. In the process your own spiritual autobiography emerges and reveals itself in the images that move you, the specific details that you see within and without.

If you began to write after reading these words, what would you be looking at? What do you see other than your own inner landscape? Do you remember the words of others that have inspired you? What do you look at and feel moved to praise God by? How do words show you what you think and what you feel? How does naming, putting words to your own experiences, lead you to see better what is outside of you? How does seeing help you to enter into the center of the landscape of your soul where you sense the nearness of God?

THERE ARE TIMES WHEN THE INTERIOR JOURNEY IS IMPEDED BY THE refusal or inability to make an external journey. The outward journey may be the move toward another person to seek forgiveness or offer forgiveness; or the journey may be toward some inner place you are afraid to enter or reenter that is closing down your world and keeping you from surrendering to God's Providence and care. The outer journey is inexplicably entwined with the inner journey and vice versa.

AND DO I find You again
in words,
did I order them right?
That order,
what does it mean,
why is anything out of order, how?
Words lose their order
in the mind
because the Word
is not received.
It is that receiving
which orders the words that
order the mind that makes
You visible again.
We have failed the first Word
and words without a beginning
are almost-words,
hints of what they are.
Write down the Word,
let it have its place
on the page
and all the words
will fall into sense,
and meaning
will no longer be a search
but a beginning.

credo

DO NOT WRITE A WORD UNTIL YOU'VE LOOKED LONG AND HARD IN the solitude of contemplation at a tree, a flower, the sea. True words arrive out of looking in prayerful solitude which is what contemplation is. Such words themselves invite contemplation, for they are both the inspiration and incarnation of a vision that is beyond that which is seen, and a yet a vision born of looking at what is seen with our bodily eyes.

These words are both my artistic credo and the bellwether that helps me determine whether or not the spirit blows through something I'm reading. The true word gestates in solitude and contemplation, for only in solitude and contemplation does the self expand and deepen, and it is out of the full self that the word emerges and names what is seen within or without. And the first word out of the first solitude is usually, "Mamma," or "Dadda," the first objects related to me as contemplative, receiving soul, the first true naming as we begin to emerge as someone related to someone or something other than ourselves.

> When I found your words, I devoured them;
> they became my joy and the happiness of my heart,
> because I bore your name,
> O LORD, God of hosts (Jeremiah 15:16, *New American Bible*)

I am struck by these words of Jeremiah who seems to say that when we devour God's words, we bear God's name. This says to me that who God is, God's very name, is the words God has given us. And all these words, as we now know, are summed up in the Incarnation, the conception and birth of Jesus Christ. The Son of God is *the* Word of God; and in becoming one of us, he gave us the most visual name of God: Jesus Christ. By extension, then, of this thought, in devouring the eucharistic Christ, we bear God's name within us.

In two ways, then, we bear God's name: by devouring symbolically the words of God, and by devouring the Body and Blood of the Incarnate Word in the Eucharist. Divine Word and Sacrament: the name of God.

What does this mean practically for my daily life? In order to bear God's name within me I have to listen to and ingest God's words as they are revealed in the Sacred Scriptures, and I must sacramentally receive the Word of God Incarnate in his Body and Blood contained in the Holy Eucharist. Only then do I know God's name and carry God in my soul and body: one God in one human being who like Jeremiah finds joy and happiness in bearing God's name.

HOW EASY IT IS TO LET OUR OWN NARROW, PREJUDICED VISION LIMIT the goodness and the magnanimous heart of God. This morning, as I read from the Dogmatic Constitution on the Church of the Second Vatican Council, these words leapt from the page as divinely inspired guidance for how we of the twenty-first century are to relate with love to others who are not of our faith. They console in a world that increasingly sees those who are different from us as "enemies."

> …Those who have not received the Gospel are in their different ways related to God's people.

> In the first place, there is that people which was given the covenants and the promises and from which Jesus Christ

was born by human descent…. God never repents of God's gifts or God's call.

God's plan of salvation embraces those also who acknowledge the Creator. Among these are especially the Muslims; they profess their faith as the faith of Abraham, and with us they worship the one, merciful God who will judge all on the last day.

God is not far from those others who seek the unknown God in darkness and shadows, for it is he who gives to all humans life and inspiration and all things, and who as Savior desires all men to be saved.

Eternal salvation is open to those who, through no fault of their own, do not know Christ and his church but seek God with a sincere heart, and under the inspiration of grace try in their lives to do God's will, made known to them by the dictates of their conscience. Nor does Divine Providence deny the aids necessary for salvation to those who, without blame on their part, have not yet reached an explicit belief in God, but strive to lead a good life, under the influence of God's grace.[1]

How urgently we need to hear these words lest religion descend to simply a human institution invented and kept going as a response to God's revelation in keeping with our own attitudes and ideas about people, life and meaning.

GOD IS NOT LIMITED BY THE RESTRICTIONS WE PLACE UPON GOD nor by our ideas and formulations of who God is, nor by the exclusion of those who differ from us.

1. Adapted from the Dogmatic Constitution on the Church, 16.

LUKE 6:27–38
As if it matters
noticing the migrant workers—
two to a wheelbarrow of concrete—
mending the walls of the rich
that exclude them

As if religion cares
not speeding past the Mexican
landscape and lawn workers
and homeless drunks
on their way to church

As if it lasts
the protest against
the long wait to enter the death chamber,
the taking of new or old or any life

As if they change anything
clouds in a blue sky that
arrest the heart
words rising from the dark cave
into the light

As if it matters
war being the outcome anyway
just or unjust
those against it mocked and crowned
with shame

As if they already possess it
the merciful
who continue to pray
and labor and protest
without counting the measure
with which they measure.

catechism

THE ROOM WAS BEHIND THE SACRISTY OF ST. FRANCIS CHURCH, Gallup, New Mexico. There, he thought, the priest who was instructing him after classes at the public grade school would show him how we know that God exists, and who this God is.

Instead, the boy's first fear, more a sort of terror, slipped from the priest's lips in the boy's private catechism class when he asked, "Who made God?" and the priest said, "No one. God has no beginning."

The boy's mind couldn't hold the words, nor imagine them, and it felt like there was no God—to have no beginning was to be nothing—and he only twelve, too young for thoughts like that and alone because he thought them.

Such thinking, though, I now know is the only true journey: the journey into nothing's no-beginning looking for something behind nothing. The fear of nothing being there is the beginning of the way in.

The fear that gripped me as a boy was that the journey from something to nothing begins not only when we die but when we begin to think of God. I was afraid that if I thought about God, I would become what God is and what God comes from: nothing. God, I feared, comes from and is nothing. This Nothing creates something from the nothing that we return to if we think or die. These were the thoughts that scared me, and later, no amount of philosophy or theology completely erased the fear engendered by them when I was twelve.

How then did the man survive the boy's thoughts? It was not through philosophy or theology but through reading in his teens the lives of the saints who looked into nothing and nothing became a person, a presence.

Often the person was Jesus Christ. Sometimes a voice, or a presence that was not nothing, but someone. So said the saints and mystics. And so he believed, for what was not his to see or hear was his to believe.

That is my faith, and the deep source of it in early manhood was the mystical dimension of reality as contained in the Bible, from the psalms to the Song of Songs to the apocalyptic Revelation of Saint John, Jesus' Beloved Disciple.

The visions of the Bible were visions of presence and person that were not visions of nothing. The eternal was not nothing but Someone that somebody like me actually saw. And that was the beginning of the faith that sustains me.

I know, for example—I don't know why, except by faith—that Peter, James and John saw a real transfiguration of the man Jesus and heard a voice from heaven that was not nothing, nor an illusion that made of nothing something.

From that humble, personal "revelation" till now, Jesus is my faith. He is the one who comes from the scary nothing. He is the someone inside the nothing, the one I would know even more intimately had I the saint's and mystic's courage to enter the terrifying nothing, believing that Jesus would be the someone inside the no-beginning of God. By grace alone do I know the little I know of God's manifestation in Jesus.

And that little is enough to take away the fear, for where he is cannot be a no-place, a nothing, but a heaven that has no beginning and no end.

The no one who became God for me is the someone who is Jesus,

Later theology taught me that God is a Trinity of Persons, equal and Divine, who though One, are in an eternal dynamic of mutual love. But I only know Jesus, whose spirit is the Holy Spirit, whose God is his Father.

Jesus is enough, being all three Persons in one personal epiphany that began shortly after a little boy being tutored by a priest became terrified that God was really no one because no one has no beginning.

> WHO CAN ever speak of You
> without the dumb catch in the heart
> before it can be spoken?
> The word ready to be released
> then leaping back into forgetfulness,
> its meaning only guessed at,
> hoped for in the silence of expectancy,
> unspoken out of time,
> beyond any human hearing.

the mystical garden

THE GARDEN OF EDEN, THE LOCKED GARDEN OF THE BRIDE IN THE
Song of Songs, the garden of Gethsemane, the new tomb in the garden where Christ rose. Images of the gardens of our own soul where
we have met God, suffered with God and, like Christ, experienced
resurrections. Gardens that we have worked the way a gardener does:
We've looked at the configuration of our inner garden, its pattern,
the constellation of plantings that have made it what it is now, its
many layers, and the depth of its soil.

As we pray and meditate, we begin to see the soul's terraces and
how they were made, how we came to a new point of our growing
that felt like something new—and was, having its own color and
texture—and yet that fit into the whole terraced structure of our life,
our metamorphosed self or perception of ourselves over the years.

The years. All has been in time and about time and yet beyond
time in the sense that some metamorphoses have taken place without our effort: They were part of the very nature bequeathed to our
soul by its Creator.

We see, too, what never really took root in us—dead withered
plants, or their remnants, like dried-up bulbs, sticks and empty
holes. We replanted some, tried again; others we gave up on, knowing that nothing would ever come of that potential or possibility;

others we saw were weeds that we thought were flowers. We rooted them out.

But the real delight is in the garden itself, what our soul has become at a given point in our life. Like God at the beginning of Genesis, we look at everything there, and see that it is good.

Our future soul-work learns a lot from this kind of taking stock of our garden. We see the organic nature of spiritual growth. Like the garden, the soul has its own built-in growth and flowering. And the work we do is only facilitating what God has already done and continues to do: We are only the gardener who reverences the soil, the plants, the seasons and weather and time itself—all are gifts of God that we reverence for the integral part they play in the shape and color and texture of whatever we tend. What we do only enhances what has already been planted before we began to work in the garden God has given us.

THE SOWN

Fallow fields empty of you
speed behind this Cisalpine
express, Geneva to Milan.
Who are you, never there, yet
always there where I look out
from the windows of my soul?
You lie in the empty fields,
The sound of your presence
silence inside barren rows.
When I turn inward, you are
there, absent as your image
standing in the fallow fields.
You are the silence of seeds
deep in the newly planted ground.
You grow where we cannot hear,

you break through the husk
beneath the level of our
hearing. You insinuate.

SOMETIMES THE BEST WAY TO PRAY IS NOT TO PRAY. IN TIMES OF PAIN or anxiety or sorrow praying might only increase the awareness of our misery and make us even more agitated or afraid. We pray in panic or desperation, bartering with God, begging God for a miracle. The harder we pray the more desperate we feel.

God already knows; God is already working. What we need to do is slow down, try to enter into quiet and breathe in God like silent air. Calm down, stop pleading, let go and receive. But receive what? I believe what we receive when we manage to calm the mind and heart is our innate capacity to give ourselves what we need. Inside us is the power to neutralize for a time whatever is causing us pain or anxiety. Even the simple act of focusing on breathing in and out slowly, rhythmically, can calm more than praying in an agitated state. Then, in the calm, the silence and peacefulness, God speaks. We hear God in the pauses, the quiet between.

mystery

WAITING IS THE MOST DIFFICULT PART OF PRAYER BECAUSE IT presupposes someone or something we are waiting for. And therefore everything is not up to us. We cannot make it happen. We can only be disposed, be ready.

What an invitation to humility! What an exercise, some may conclude, in futility! For, unlike a relaxation exercise, or even some prayer-practices, the prayer I am referring to here is not a performance of rituals or postures that guarantee some kind of tangible result like illumination or heightened awareness. All that this prayer guarantees is patient watchfulness and readiness to receive the touches of God when they are given.

> I REACH around the mystery
> of You, trying to hold onto
> something beyond myself.
> But You keep fleeing
> from my grasp like
> a phantom of my own
> desires. And then
> I stop and let You
> come to me and all Your
> mystery is tangible

and real, a light
bright presence
in my selfish arms.
How is it with You, Lord?
I'm waiting here
a little bored.

HOW IS IT, LORD, THAT YOU WHO ARE SO CLOSE TO ME ARE SO FAR away and what I know of you is mainly your absence? I see the faces of your presence in my life: those virtues I see in others and know they are not their virtues but yours, those surprising acts of love people don't know they have it in them to enact. But your nearness in power that is beyond us is farness of seeing you.

I want to reach out to you, and do so in prayer, but the arms of my prayer find only air. At times you're generous, and there is a movement of my heart I cannot explain, a sort of movement through my heart as if someone passed through it leaving a kind of warmth that at times flames up in desire. A desire for you who are the absence of whatever it was that stirred my heart. Was it you? I sit in silence, I hold my breath so as not to lose whatever it was that momentarily brushed my heart like a kiss.

I exhale and feel myself being inhaled. I try to find words to understand, for I only know with words. Yet words, too, seem a further farness of what I'm trying to hold onto.

What mystery is here! A further farness: mystery. As close as the word is, for example, it is far from what it names which has already passed, though we think it is as near as the word that names it.

And so I let go of my will to hold on to what was given and withdrawn freely, apart from me. I wait in silence, I try to still my heart, knowing only that my acceptance of your absence will bring you near; only in silent surrender to your farness do you draw near and stir my heart, drawing me out of myself into the absence that is your nearness. For only in being Other, apart from me, can you visit me, dwell in me, without your presence being only my illusion, my need for you to be there, rather than your real visitation, you who are not me or my desire for you.

You are apart, separate, far; and because you are that farness, you can be the nearness I experience when you choose to come to me without my seeing you who stir my heart. How that is, I don't know. That is the mystery.

1.
HERE IN the dark
I begin to see things
I want to see; I hear
the song of Your coming
and rise up with wings
poised for ecstasy.
But my visions disappear
with snickers
sinister in the silence.

2.
The shuddering dark is all.
I cower till morning light
waiting for Your warm return.
You are light and come with light.
The darkness is ours or theirs
who laugh derisively at us
helpless in the dark they fill
with our own doubt and fear
disenfleshed, inspirited.

3.
You do not watch.
You appear and disappear

like light. You love.
You trust me when You leave.
You send no one to tempt me.
You know that if they come,
they will come from me
afraid to face your leaving.
4.
Light shines in darkness
from within
when praise replaces watching,
when watching over and watching for
become unnecessary to dispel the demons
of the solitary night,
when the eye through the darkness
sees the light,
when the heart alone
feels the warm approaching,
when a far, weak star suffices.

the will of god

"Thy will be done on earth as it is in heaven."

GOD'S WILL HINGES ON THE SEEMINGLY IMPOSSIBLE, FOR IT IS GOD'S will to become one of us. The will of God is Jesus Christ, the descent of God to us who cannot go to God except in him who first came to us.

The will of God is revealed in Jesus Christ, who is both in heaven and on earth. We don't know God's will fully except as that will is made known in the Incarnation. And so we pray that God's will be done on earth as it is in heaven. What Christ does here in time is what he does in heaven in eternity. He is the outpouring love of the Holy Trinity made impossibly concrete for us. And we know this only by his gift of the Holy Spirit, who enables us to know what otherwise would be impossible to know: namely, the descent and ascent of God in Jesus Christ.

That is why, for Christians, it is all about Jesus Christ, who in his Spirit reveals to us the will of our Father who is in heaven. This is clotted stuff to write about, but simple stuff to know once the Holy Spirit illumines who Jesus Christ really is. Then his words and his actions become the revelation of God in our world. God's will is done in Jesus, for it is God's will to be not only one with us, but one of us, so that we might be one with God.

Jesus prays further that we might be one with one another as he is one with the Father (see John 17:21). That is his will for us, he who is the Son of the Father. Saint Paul makes this will of God concrete for us in his image of the mystical body of Christ (see 1 Corinthians 12:12–14).

images

EVIL IS SO EMBODIED IN THIS WORLD THAT GOD HAD TO COME TO us embodied. Otherwise, God would have been pure Spirit removed from us, and we would have known only Evil as the embodied one.

The Incarnation is the embodiment of God and henceforth we would know pure goodness, and we would know besides what we can become and already are, if only we open ourselves to him who is our image, just as he is the image of the invisible God.

JESUS, YOU WHO ARE THE IMAGE OF WHO I AM, LET ME SEE THAT truth in my life, help me to know that like you I am made in the image of God. And as God's image I can be the embodiment of God in my world and my time. Shine through me, beautiful, loving God.

SHE WOULD SIT AT THE END OF THE DOCK EACH MORNING AND look out at the bay. She would stay, usually, about a half hour, then return to her day's work. When I asked why she sat on the dock, still and pensive, each morning, she said, "I don't wake up a nun. I wake up a human being like everyone else. I come out here to recommit myself to being a nun."

Our daily prayer is like that. We set apart time at the beginning of the day to recommit ourselves to our calling, our vocation, or to ask for enlightenment to know what our vocation is. Much of who we become depends on the willingness to commit ourselves to something larger than ourselves that gives meaning and direction to a life that otherwise is directed from outside, by every fad and pressure, to become what others want us to be, rather than what we want to be.

We know who we really are by listening in silence to our own inner movement and then committing ourselves to directing that movement toward something that makes of our inner movement more than self-serving self-fulfillment. That is the paradox: We move inward to discern our own inner movement, but we have to move outward to keep that inner movement from turning in upon itself.

The nun on the dock is an image of this dynamic. She enters the silence and solitude of her morning prayer, not in order to stay there, but to find there a way of bringing her recommitment to her vocation to the world around her. She has to remind herself who she is if she is to be who she is for herself and others.

You do not wake up a husband or wife, a mother or father, a son or daughter; a single person living in the world, a priest, a brother, a nun, a sister. You wake up a human being who has to remember and recommit to being what your decisions and your life have made you.

> AT LEAST twice when I was thinking
> of nothing in particular, something
> cohered in me. Light beyond the light
> I saw outside me (though it, too, was
> enhanced) convinced me this instant
> was it, whatever "it" was—this peace,
> this feeling of wholeness, contentment,
> though I was only leaning each time
> on a windowsill watching a Summer
> day become perfect Summer inside me.

assisi rising

IT WAS THE YEAR SAINT FRANCIS FOUND ME ON THE VIA GALEAZZO Alessi in Assisi. His voice merged with mine and the words began to pour onto the page and the poppies began to bloom in the fields below my window.

That was 1972, the year I thought my life as a priest and a friar was coming to an end. Then Saint Francis found me and it was all reenkindled, that love of the Poverello and of the Poor Christ, and I knew the words would come and from them would come the healing.

That was the year nervous exhaustion threatened my continuing as a public person in the church and written words began to do what talking does in therapy: The words on the page entered into and flowed from the soul which in turn began to expand and refill the empty places, to surround and warm the broken places.

That was the year Assisi entered my soul.

What happens when a place that is more than a place enters the soul? It peoples the soul with the people outside and inside time, which is what makes Assisi the mystical city it is. Francis and Clare are there and all the Brothers and Poor Ladies and all the good people who followed in the footsteps of the saints of Assisi. What was past becomes present, what was far away is close, and the souls of the saints begin to speak.

To have lived in Assisi for thirty years of summers is to have shared a bit of paradise and, like the world in and around that

Umbrian hill town, a bit of something that is eroding from commercialism and kitsch, too. And yet... it is still there, the intangible spirit of Francis and Clare, the indomitable man and woman, bonded in Christ to each other and to all those who follow in their footsteps.

San Damiano, the chapel Francis restored with his own hands and where Clare lived for forty-one years, is a symbol of the animus and anima of the Franciscan soul, of Francis and Clare conjoined in their contemplation of the San Damiano crucifix, the cross that spoke to Francis and the cross Clare contemplated her whole life long at San Damiano. Her mirror she called it: the Crucified Christ as mirror of who she and all the Poor Ladies were to become.

In Clare's life the mirror of the crucifix became most real to her in the long illness she endured, bedridden much of the time, for some twenty-one years. Yet, even in suffering she served her sisters, often rising from her bed to minister to their needs, especially those who were themselves ill.

Her penances, too, were so severe that they were a kind of crucifixion. In fact, Francis had to admonish her to be more merciful toward her own body. But Clare's penances and sufferings were not, as is sometimes thought of the saints, a form of masochism. They were rather a response of love to a Love that, because of human sin, had to suffer and die that sin would lose its hold on us and all our sins might be forgiven.

The penances of saints like Clare are also an attempt to join with Christ's redemptive suffering. Clare knew that we all have been reconciled once and for all by Christ, but to enter into that redemptive suffering, and even to lay down one's life for others, makes God's presence among us evident in our own times. Christ died once and for all, but to enter voluntarily into that sacrifice with Christ out of love of God and neighbor, effects a further outpouring of grace among believers and strengthens the faith of those whose faith is waning. This selfless pouring out of one's life for others for love of Christ can, of course, only be done in God's grace; it is *the* sign of Christ's continuing presence among us. It was so for Clare; it is so for us today.

SAINT CLARE IN CONTEMPLATION

"Eternal Beatitude is a state where to look is to eat."

—Simone Weil

Silence
Her silence lifts
the vestment of God,
uncovers
what is already there,
like the silence
of that voice on the cross
uncovering the soundless
Word of God.
Breath
To be inhaled by God
is to inhale the breath
she thinks
she's surrendered.
Bread
The quiet and vulnerable
Sacrament.
In surrender
to this bread
she becomes as silent
as the God who surrenders
to her hunger.
Beatitude
She herself becomes

the silent bread
her sisters eat.

THE MYSTIC SAINT CLARE

I strained from womb to womb,
each passage leaving the tomb
behind that I thought was all
there was, a world as small
as what it hid, enclosed.

Just as I supposed,
when I died, the strain
upon the merest membrane
broke the tissue of night;
I fell into light within light.

THE TOWN OF FOLIGNO LIES IN THE VALLEY QUITE NEAR ASSISI. IT IS
the town to which Saint Francis fled at the beginning of his conversion to sell a bolt of cloth and his father's horse for money to repair
the little chapel of San Damiano. It was also the town of the
medieval Franciscan Tertiary and mystic, Blessed Angela of Foligno,
who said, "The world is great with God." Whatever Blessed Angela
intended by that, I like to think she meant, the world is pregnant
with God, and we are here to bring God forth in our midst. We are
to bring forth a God who first brought us to birth.

By becoming human, God was bringing every human being to
rebirth in God. And not only humans but the world, too, and all of
creation.

This is a deep mystery: God becomes what God first created so
that God's creation might become a worthy return of God's love.
God's love in creating the universe is infinite and therefore only God
can return that love to the Blessed Trinity, so the Second Person of the
Trinity enters God's creation to return the very love that created it.

By becoming one of God's creatures in Jesus Christ, God subsumes all of creation in this one creature, Jesus, who is himself the very God who created him. What mystery is here!

Jesus Christ is, therefore, as Saint Paul says, the firstborn of the Father and of all of us, his brothers and sisters in his one Body. He is the head and we the body of God, so that in one sense, God is all of us in Jesus Christ.

One could meditate on this mystery for a lifetime; for in this mystery is the whole beautiful truth of who we really are beneath our sinfulness and imperfection. We are the Body of God.

> FRANCIS
> He is the one
>   in dreams,
> hooded,
>   medieval.
> He draws scrolls
>   from a basket.
> He has
>   no name.
> He hands
>   me
>   the scrolls.
> I can't
>   see
>   his face.
> I write
>   between
>   the lines.

SAINT FRANCIS USED TO OBSERVE WITH INEXPRESSIBLE eagerness and above all other solemnities, the Birth of the Child Jesus, calling it the feast of feasts wherein God, having become a little baby, hung upon human breasts. He would avidly kiss pictures of those infant limbs, and his compassion for the child overflowed his heart, making him stammer sweet words, even like a child. The name Baby Jesus was for him honeycomb-sweet in the mouth.

—Blessed Brother Thomas of Celano,
the first biographer of Saint Francis

EVERY YEAR IN CINCINNATI'S EDEN PARK THERE IS A LIVE CHRISTMAS crèche. The stable is built in late November, and at the beginning of Advent live sheep, a donkey and cow, and sometimes a little goat, surround manikins of Mary and Joseph and the Child Jesus. Once when I was praying at this sweet scene, it struck me that though the animals are alive, the figures of the Holy Family are not. And suddenly I remembered the words of Saint Francis that we are the ones who bring the Holy Family to life in our own lives and in our own time. Jesus, Mary and Joseph become real in our lives when we, like Mary, give birth to Jesus, when, like Joseph, we care for the Son of God who has been placed in our care in every baby who is born.

Saint Francis tells us how this is done when he says in his "Letter to the Faithful" that we are called to become spouses, brothers and sisters, and mothers of our Lord Jesus Christ. He writes:

We are spouses when our soul is joined by the Holy Spirit to our Lord Jesus Christ. We are brothers and sisters to him when we do the will of our Father in Heaven. We are mothers when we carry him lovingly in our hearts and bodies, and with a pure and sincere conscience, and give birth to him through the working of his grace in us which should shine forth in holy actions that are an example to others.

HOW TRANSFORMED OUR LIVES WOULD BE IF WE WOULD BECOME these words of Saint Francis. And not only would our own lives be changed but so would the lives of those with whom we come into contact.

poetry

POETRY IS NOT A PRETTIFICATION OF LIFE; POETRY IS LIFE, A WAY OF articulating the marvelous union of soul and body, spirit and matter. In true poetry the word becomes flesh. In a thing made of words is the spirit of God. The poet's way is a way of connecting heaven and earth, spirit and matter, one human being and another, human beings and nature, a human being with her or his self. And all this connecting is done through images made of words.

This image-making is especially important today in our spin-doctor, wag-the-dog world that serves up violent, skewed and ugly images and bombards us with them daily. And "bombards" is the word here. Not only the literal bombs that fall from the sky on inno-cent people, but the figurative bombs of lies, half-truths, deception, and all the other evil that comes out of the human heart. The images that keep us from being pure of heart are the images that derive from the evil of the human heart. Images, as Jesus says, that defile us. "For it is from within," Jesus says, "from the human heart, that evil inten-tions come: fornication, theft, murder, adultery, avarice, wickedness, deceit, licentiousness, envy, slander, pride, folly. All these things come from within, and they defile a person" (Mark 7:21–23).

What comes from within results in actions that become images in the minds of those who witness them, those who suffer them, and those who perpetrate them. Saint James points out a few of these actions and images in his Letter:

> Where do these wars and battles between yourselves first start? Is it not precisely in the desires fighting inside your own selves? You want something and you lack it; so you kill. You have an ambition that you cannot satisfy; so you fight to get your way by force. It is because you do not pray that you do not receive; when you do pray and do not receive, it is because you prayed wrongly, wanting to indulge your passions. (James 4:13)

It is the task of the Christian poet to name the images of these passions, to see into how they are transformed by the power of Christ that takes our twisted, perverted images and becomes incarnate in them by taking on our human nature and by entering into our world in order that evil might be transformed by the infinite goodness and light of his Divinity. As Saint John says at the beginning of his gospel, "The light shines in the darkness, and the darkness did not overcome it" (John 1:5).

This transforming of images is not something only the poet can do. In fact, the poet does not do it; the poet names the transformations he or she sees in the world. Every person can become a transformed image if only one lets God do the transforming. It is what Saint Francis of Assisi was about his whole life long.

He allowed God to transform the image of a rich and spoiled, extravagantly dressed young man into a poor beggar whose once bejeweled hands reached out and bathed the wounds of lepers. He allowed God to transform a young man who loved nature in itself into a man who saw in nature the image of the good God. He allowed God to transform a young man who sang secular love songs into the first great Italian poet who praised God through all that God has made, who took the four elements of the universe: earth, water, air and fire, and praised God through them calling them Brother Wind and Sister Water, Brother Fire and Sister Earth our mother.

What are the images of our world that have been skewed and turned to purposes other than what God intended them to be? What has become deformed and ugly and needs the Franciscan vision to see it aright again?

Saint Bonaventure says that justice makes beautiful that which has been deformed. What is it in our world that is deformed and needs justice to make it beautiful again? Saint Francis made beautiful the face of thirteenth century leprosy by embracing lepers and seeing Christ in them. What do we need to embrace in Christ in order that its face may be made beautiful by our love, our vision of Christ within what we thought was repulsive? Perhaps we need to begin, as Saint Francis did, with ourselves and embrace ourselves and see the beauty there first of all.

SPARROW
There is this bird
which is this now,
this brown sparrow
outside my window.
Sparrow who is its history:
everything wrong with its
dull brown, its diseases,
is its history which is now.
Its good is its history.
Its song and seemingly
endless propagation
is history's now:
bright tones of brown.

THIS JOURNAL IS COMING TO AN END AND I UNDERSTAND WHY. IT IS dying of itself, so I suppose there is no more to say, or at least that I have nothing more to say. It is unsatisfying somehow, and yet it is complete because there is no more. You can only listen to a sparrow so long, and perhaps this is already much more of sparrow-talk than anyone can bear. So I will quit on the bright brown notes of this last poem.

P.S. I haven't seen a sparrow for a while. Too much indoor living and indoor writing. Now it is time for you and me to go outdoors and let nature and people free us from ourselves. It is time to take to the road again.

> THE SECRET of life on the road
> is not to get there before you're there
> and not to live in the place you've left
> while you're on the way.

afterword

A BOOK LIKE THIS MAY GIVE THE IMPRESSION OF REPRODUCING THE actual prayer life of the author. Perhaps it does, but only indirectly. For the writer, the poet, enters into himself or herself (often painfully) to create some order out of a confused and sometimes chaotic inner life. This is an intensely self-conscious kind of activity and as such is the very opposite of prayer which actually frees one from self-consciousness and introspection. True prayer is a liberating experience and has nothing to do with navel-gazing and a heightened awareness of the self. Rather the self is "lost" in contemplation of the other, in wonder at what is not itself.

These poems and meditations, then, although they grew out of moments of heightened awareness, do not really represent or reproduce my own prayer experience. For one's prayer life is in a sense inexpressible and can at most be hinted at through symbols that merely approximate the real experience. Because the use of symbols is a conscious and reflective act, the real prayer experience is lost. For when we pray, we do not watch ourselves praying or analyze what is happening or think how we are going to communicate our experience to others. We merely surrender our deepest self to the Spirit and lose ourselves in God.

It is only after prayer or in periods of darkness that the mind tries to remember symbolically how it was and what it was that happened. Many of these poems and meditations, for example, are exercises of the creative process that goes on between the real experiences of God. They are like doodles that artists make or songs that singers sing while they are waiting for the muse or for the Spirit to free them from self-conscious activity and enable them to be lost again in contemplation of something or someone other than themselves. They are meant to fill in the time with human meaning until something happens and God returns again.